Basic Sculptural Modeling:

Developing the Will by Working with Pure Forms in the First Three Grades

Basic Sculptural Modeling:

Developing the Will by Working with Pure Forms in the First Three Grades

by
Hella Loewe

Introduction by
Arthur F. Auer

Translation by
Karin DiGiacomo

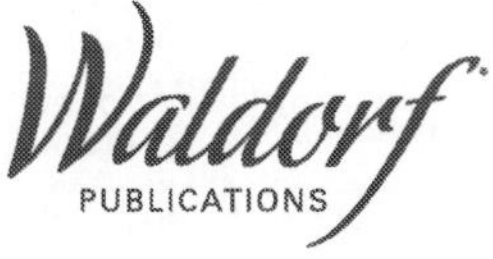

Printed with support from the Waldorf Curriculum Fund

Published by:
Waldorf Publications at the
Research Institute for Waldorf Education
38 Main Street
Chatham, NY 12037

Title: *Basic Sculptural Modeling:*
   Developing the Will by Working with Pure Forms in the First Three Grades
Author: Hella Loewe
Translator: Karin DiGiacomo
Photography: Andreas Burz
Editor: David Mitchell
Proofreader: Ann Erwin
Cover: Hallie Wootan
© 2006 by AWSNA
ISBN # 1-978-888365-73-3

First edition in German 2004, published by NWWP, Stuttgart, Germany
Original ISBN # 3-9808485-8-2
Quotations from Rudolf Steiner are printed with the kind permission of the Rudolf Steiner Verlag,
Dornach, Switzerland

TABLE OF CONTENTS

FOREWORD

Sculptural modeling *should begin before the ninth year*, first with spheres, then other forms and so on. Also, with modeling one should work entirely out of the forms.

Rudolf Steiner, *Discussions with Teachers*, Lecture XV, p. 178

Awaken in the children the feeling for form before the urge to imitate outer objects awakens. Wait until later before allowing them to apply what they have practiced in drawing forms to imitating actual objects. First have them draw angles so that they understand what an angle is through its shape... Do not let children imitate anything until they have cultivated their feeling for forms standing independently on their own. Things can be imitated later. Stick to this principle even when you move on to a more independent and creative treatment of drawing, painting and modeling.

Rudolf Steiner, "Second Curriculum Lecture" in *Discussions with Teachers,* p. 199

When children enter the *first and second grade*, [emphasis by AA] they are perfectly able to make this transition from play into artistic channels. However clumsy children of six or seven may be when modeling, painting, or finding their way into music and poetry, if teachers know how to permeate their lessons with artistry, even young children as young sculptors or painters can begin to have the experience that human nature does not end at the fingertips, that is, at the periphery of the skin, but flows out into the world. *The adult human being is growing in first and second grade children whenever they put their being into handling clay,* [emphasis by AA] wood, or paints. In these very interactions with materials, children grow, learning to perceive how closely the human being is interwoven with the fabric of the world. These [artistic activities] permit a freedom of inner activity while at the same time forcing the children to struggle with outer materials, as we have to do in adult work.

Rudolf Steiner, *Waldorf Education and Anthroposophy*, vol. 2, pp. 58–59

The founder of Waldorf education, Rudolf Steiner intended sculptural modeling (*plastisches Gestalten*) to be one of the three main artistic pillars of a visual arts curriculum along with drawing and painting. Furthermore, he wanted the modeling of pure forms to be practiced with young children before they were too strongly inclined to make naturalistic figures. He recommended that this approach start with basic archetypal geometric forms such as the sphere. Young children benefit significantly from shaping little sculptural forms in clay that initially need not represent any 'thing' in the world. 'Playing' creatively with changing, non-representational shapes stimulates a child's sense of form and imagination in educationally valuable ways. While pure color painting (color stories) and pure form drawing have been widely practiced in the early grades in Waldorf schools, Steiner's indications for what can be called pure form modeling have not been generally taken up, although like an open secret, they have been clearly published for over eighty years.

In 2000, as I was finishing *Learning about the World through Modeling: Sculptural Ideas for School and Home* (AWSNA Publications, Fair Oaks, CA, 2001), I began to realize the educational potential of certain of Steiner's 'overlooked' indications on the modeling of abstract forms. I was particularly inspired by several such exercises developed along these lines by Anke-Usche Clausen and Martin Riedel (*Plastisches Gestalten,* Mellinger Verlag, 1985). At the last minute, I managed to include a few examples of this new pedagogical direction for the younger grades in my new manual. (I have subsequently been working on a sequel called *Pure Form Modeling.*) It was a real joy then at that same time to suddenly encounter a fellow class teacher and colleague across the Atlantic who was not only thinking the same thoughts, but who had been successfully practicing form modeling with her class for several years. Hella Loewe, now retired from the Waldorf school at Kräherwald in Stuttgart, Germany, first reported on her pioneering work in an article (with photographs) on "Modeling in the Early Grades—A Research Report on Classroom Practice" (*German Waldorf Teachers' Newsletter,* November 2000). This initial report, which I translated into English, became the seed for the present book four years later. It is a superb example of a dedicated teacher who enhances her professional service to her children by carrying out action research of the highest caliber. This special initiative was also an act of courage on her part, for, as Hella Loewe writes:

"To work with clay in the first grade was at that time – as far as I knew – not customary in Waldorf schools; some class teachers did let the students of the first and second grades form small figurines in beeswax. But only a few teachers regarded the clay modeling of elementary, abstract forms in the first three to four grades as part of the art curriculum and it was rarely done. Considering this background I am very grateful to the former faculty of the Independent Waldorf School at Kräherwald; they gave me express permission to take this unusual path with the children of the first three grades. My colleagues followed my work and constructively questioned it – especially in the beginning phase – with very critical, and at the same time very well-meaning, interest. A small group of colleagues started meeting shortly after

I began to do clay modeling with the children; the members of this group agreed to participate cooperatively in a pedagogical research project in the field of clay modeling in the first three grades. [Joining] us were three professors who were working in the area of sculptural-pictorial arts. All three of them encouraged me to do what I thought to be right and what experience required for these children with whom I was entrusted, independent of what was customary."

In this book Hella Loewe describes a marvelous series of exercises that she found met the needs and challenges of the rambunctious and spirited children in her care. She discovered that these exercises in clay invigorate the life forces and circulation of her children in the early grades and harmonize their disparate impulses. The organic forms she developed arose wonderfully out of the natural movements and configurations of the children's hands themselves. The children became aware of the transforming capabilities of their own spirit-permeated hands. Modeling as a direct contact art imparted a great healing effect on the class. Unmediated by brush, crayon, or other utensil, this primal human activity engages the whole hand and both hands together, directly sensing and feeling the clay of the good earth. In so doing, it engaged the whole child, the whole class.

Working first with pure forms before tackling natural figures is not only a good preparation in learning artistic fundamentals but also good stimulation for creativity and inventiveness. Children at times feel intimidated by what a naturalistic subject is supposed to look like and even disappointed if their efforts fall short. Modeling pure forms is less constraining and it lends itself more freely into the discovery of new forms. Form modeling has a freeing effect on a child's attitude and enables him or her to become readily involved in the lively flow of an exciting process that leads into the unknown and unexpected. Like form drawing, sculpting forms continues to vibrate in the unconscious at night and vitalize inner capacities.

Hella Loewe associates the excitement and anticipation that children exhibit in the sculptural modeling process with the gesture of reaching out to an emerging and unfolding future. This stands in contrast to creating out of what one knows from the past, what is relatively fixed and given. She refers to a mode of artistic engagement that deeply fires the will out of sense of discovery of something new:

"I would like to designate the pedagogical stream that activates and strengthens the will forces of children as the 'stream of the future' in the sculptural-pictorial realm. In contrast to this, we can speak of a stream that the children bring with them, the 'stream of the past' that becomes visible in the illustrative drawings and paintings of children and in the little representational figures they model. This stream gradually exhausts itself. It is important that we clearly distinguish the underlying character of the different artistic activities we teach the children."

"Modeling in the Early Grades"
*German Waldorf Teachers'
Newsletter*, November 2000

Both streams in my mind – past and future – live in the children. On the one hand, youngsters are naturally attracted to drawing or modeling figures that help them represent and process their outer and inner experiences. Children re-member, re-activate, and re-live the forms of the world which they already have as archetypes within their souls from a past, prebirth existence. Modeling helps them to re-cognize through an artistic medium what they are waking up to in the world "out of a sleep and a forgetting." (See *Learning about the World through Modeling* by the author). On the other hand, modeling pure universal forms enables children to experience a complementary 'stream of the future' coming towards them with new and as yet unrealized potential. They benefit immensely when they encounter the universal workshop of pure forms. The sense and feeling for form gained in this new dimension helps them at a later age penetrate phenomena and objects in the natural world. Consciousness of the *past* is complemented by the warm new energy of reaching out to the *future* as children come to themselves gradually in the *present*.

Today's students are calling out for the excitement and anticipation of exploring new forms and the deep and formative hands-on experiences that sculptural modeling with clay uniquely provides. They long to exercise freely the intelligence of their hands in earthly substance, to feel its challenging resistance and to see what emerges anew each time. Exerting their action- or so-called will- (volitional) intelligence releases new energy and naturally charges the learning process with emotion and life. Exercising this magical fusion of the feeling-will builds and underpins real and *whole*-some intelligence. More than ever before, our young people are showing us that they wish to be whole human beings of hand, heart and head. They do not want to just think ideas but feel and act on them. They want to meet 'the stream of the future.' Hella Loewe's book is an excellent guide for teachers to help their students on their individual paths in that direction!

– Arthur Auer, M.Ed.
Antioch University
Waldorf Teacher Education

Introduction
to the First German Edition

This book is the fruit of years of artistic-therapeutic work as a class teacher at a Waldorf school, where I always engaged the class as a whole in this kind of art therapy during main lesson periods. Children of a first grade class gave the key impulse for developing this work, which was very uncommon in the lower grades until then. Those children showed particularly disruptive behaviors, making it very difficult to teach in an ordered manner. I was challenged to find ways and means to channel and strengthen the will of these children in applications that were appropriate for their age and that would provide them with discipline without pressure or punishment.

In this situation I decided to do sculptural modeling with clay, because I had myself experienced the beneficial and harmonizing effects of sculpting with clay.[1] I hoped it would help some individual children and also the class as a whole.

When Rudolf Steiner founded the Independent Waldorf School in 1919 and so initiated Waldorf education, he strongly emphasized how important it was to foster the artistic energy in children from an early age on. "The Artistic Energy has indeed a very special effect on the will aspect of man."[2] His concept in the sculptural-pictorial arts classes for the lower grades included right from the beginning form drawing, watercolor painting and the sculptural modeling of pure forms. These three disciplines were supposed to form one integrated whole. He gave the teachers many detailed instructions and concrete examples in regard to form drawing and painting. Both of these artistic disciplines have become a regular part of the Waldorf curriculum. Steiner left relatively few remarks about sculptural modeling for the first few grades of school, and unfortunately no concrete examples. Perhaps that is why sculptural modeling has not been incorporated into the curriculum.

Steiner says that during the change of teeth the child "has definitively the urge to create three-dimensional forms."[3] Further, "modeling should start before the ninth year. Also, with modeling, one should work entirely out of the forms."[4]

The experiences described herein are in part based on the previously mentioned practical work and in part on the work of a research group that explored sculptural modeling of pure forms during the first school years. This work may contribute to including sculptural modeling in its rightful pedagogical place in the schools, side by side with form drawing and painting, benefiting many children and bringing them joy as well as healing from the challenges of our time.

The changes in the social and cultural conditions in our highly technical world, in which today's children are growing up, often result in their needs of soul and spirit no longer being met. The increased pressure towards competition and being political correct not only impact their home life, but even preschool programs and certainly the elementary schools. As a result of the International PISA study, curricula have been restructured and the pressure to achieve has become more intense for children of all age groups. Therefore, it is ever more important to work towards permeating all lessons with artistic elements.

Another grave encroachment on the healthy development of today's children is, as we all know, the influence of electronic media. Their damaging effects have been presented and repeatedly proven by a variety of scientific studies.[5] Nowadays, respon-sible adults have to consciously look for alternatives in order to counteract the urge of children towards the lifeless virtual world which is ever so easily accessed with the push of a button.

That can be accomplished by reconnecting the children with the 'fountains of life.' There are various possible ways to do that, but it is primarily by artistic means that we can bring to bear a balancing, helping and healing influence. The less today's children are able to creatively use their limbs, especially their hands, the more we need to inspire them towards meaningful but non-utilitarian artistic activities. For truly, only one's own intense activity can develop into lasting faculties and abilities.

Specifically sculptural modeling allows the children to access the creative spirit and the developmental processes of nature and art in a special way. Sculpting contributes to keen spatial sensitivity in the child and trains the hands in their complex faculties to sense and grasp forms. Sculptural modeling helps develop the sense of touch and thereby not only promotes language acquisition[6] but also helps strengthen the child's self-confidence.

Several shorter reports of mine about sculptural modeling with the lower grades have been published in 2000 and 2001 in two pedagogical journals and one medical-pedagogical magazine. The vivid interest of numerous readers has encouraged me to offer now a more extensive presentation. For their valuable, insightful advice regarding the work at hand, I give heartfelt thanks to Hilde Berthold-Andrae, Matthias Karutz, Dr. Ernst-Michael Kranich, Gottfried Lesch and Dr. Claudia McKeen. My cordial thanks also go to Andreas Burz, who took photographs of the clay forms with artistic sensitivity, and Hubert Weiss whose design assembled all text and picture materials into an artful integrated whole.

Last but not least, I want to cordially thank my son, Jens Loewe, for energetically assuring a speedy publication of the book.

– Hella Loewe
Stuttgart, October 2004

The spherical form as a primordial life form is the starting point
for all form transformations pictured and described herein. In
the sphere, the forces radiating from the periphery inwards are in
balance with those emanating from the center outward.

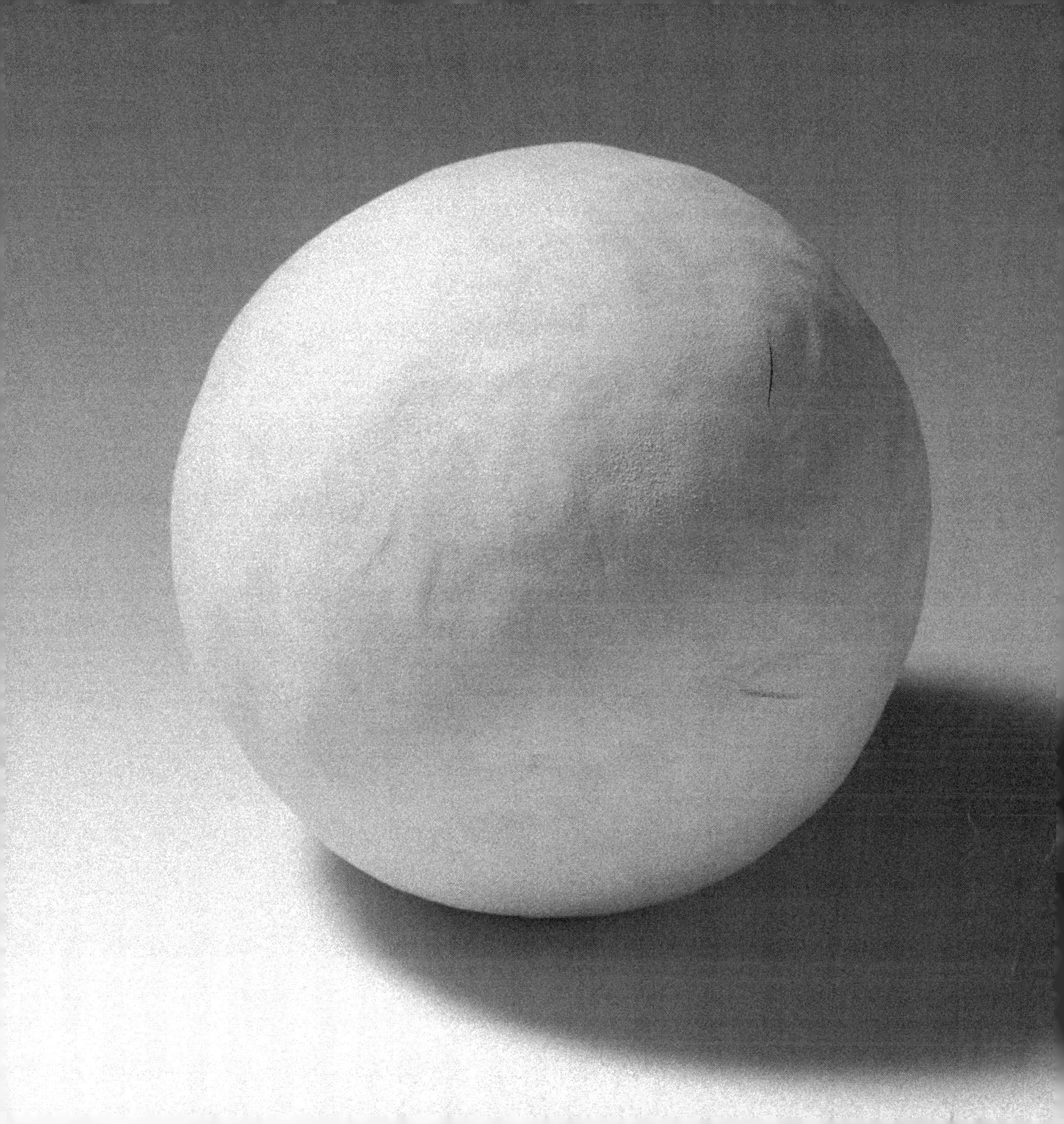

I

FROM PRACTICAL SCHOOL EXPERIENCE
MODELING WITH CLAY IN FIRST GRADE

The classrooms for the first two grades are situated on the second floor of the "Old Villa" where the Kräherwald Waldorf School in Stuttgart, Germany, was founded more than fifty years ago. It is the end of January, a Monday morning, at about 7:30 AM. It is still dark outside, a cold wind blows around the house. In the classroom, the teacher has prepared everything for welcoming her children – twenty-one boys and eighteen girls have been entrusted to her care in this class – her third class track.

The first children come, scurrying and rumbling and stomping up the old, wide wooden staircase, and enter the classroom where their teacher welcomes them. Right away a few children ask, "Oh, are we making forms again today?" "May I pass out the clay?" "Yeah, making forms is much better than even painting!" Happy noises abound. Just as in painting class, the children don their aprons and frocks and take their seats with amazing swiftness. The chairs are not arranged in the morning circle, but stand behind the desks just like on painting day. After a short tussle by the door, even the wildest and most rambunctious boys find their places quickly. A joyous readiness permeates the classroom.

At a sign from the class teacher, all children get up and fold their hands for the daily morning verse, "The Sun with loving light makes bright for me each day…" sounds into the world full of vigor and trust. And while they go on to sing a morning song together, the sun indeed rises and shines through the classroom windows.

An idealized picture? Does such a scene still exist today in a classroom with nearly forty children? On a table in front of the class by the blackboard sits the magic medium for this expectant group of children, who follow their teacher as a matter of course. It is hidden under damp cloths: forty little mounds of fine, white clay.

The teacher-appointed volunteer helpers – there is never any lack for these – quietly put a wooden art board in front of each child, followed by a portion of clay. Now the children wait, full of excitement for the moment when they can start. This is really a test of patience; the beautiful damp clay in front of them entices, urges them to take it into their hands! But one of the golden rules which they practice over and over and learn to keep says that they must wait until each child has received his or her portion. When the teacher takes her own lump of clay into her hands, that signals the beginning.

"Let us first try out how the clay feels today!" And just like the teacher, the children hold the clay to their cheeks and feel how it is quite cold. "Now you portion off a little piece of your clay and put it aside. Next, we want to feel our way through the rest of the clay, bit by bit, very gently. Delicately we use the tips of our thumbs, index and middle fingers, to explore the clay gently through and through and prepare it for our work that way. If you find a little stone or a hair in the clay, quietly put it aside."

Right away, the children start to work busily and quietly. One of our most important golden rules for forming practice is: "The mouth is silent while the hands do the work!" Soon a sense of well-being permeates the classroom. The children, just like the teacher, stack the flat little pieces of clay which are now thoroughly worked through. Every once in a while they compress the stacked pieces with the flat

of their hand, so that the clay does not dry out. After all the children have carefully felt their way through the clay, they follow the teacher's instructions and pick it up and take it into both hands, just as she does, but the piece previously portioned off remains on the board. They squeeze the clay, so that they can just enfold the lump with both hands while the wrists (carpal bones) touch each other. Now the teacher goes around making sure that each child has just the right amount of clay in relation to his or her hand size, so they can just barely encircle the lump. That means, the fingers of the child's right and left hands no longer touch, if possible. Otherwise there would be too little clay for freely handling the work.

The children sit upright in their chairs, at a distinct distance from their desks. The feet remain flat on the floor. The teacher stands in front of her class and begins to form her clay; the children follow. She holds it approximately level with her heart area, enfolds it in both hands and squeezes it in turn first with the right hand, then with the left hand, compressing it vigorously. She turns the lump each time a little bit to apply even pressure all around. She makes sure that her shoulders and arms stay relaxed, in which posture she can feel her way into movements that are rhythmic and at the same time vigorous. Most children unconsciously imitate the relaxed posture of the teacher and freely move their arms and elbows. If a child were to press his elbows close to the body, he no longer would be able to breathe and work freely. If all goes well, the children take up the teacher's movements spontaneously, moving in unison with her, as is the natural tendency at this age level.

The teacher might say, "I move the clay back and forth between my two hands and squeeze it vigorously. Now I can feel how the clay presses against both my hands from within. I form the clay with my hollow hands. I make it round, while I turn it again and again. Now my thumb slowly explores the clay surface, becomes aware of the uneven spots; it pushes, smoothes, moves a little clay into the hollowed areas and evens them out that way." Then she keeps working silently.

Meanwhile the lumps of clay becomes rounder and rounder in the hands of the teacher and of most of the children, towards a harmonious form. (It can happen that a child is not able to round out her clay – even after repeated practice – that she cannot fully create the form. In this case the teacher can help out.) The teacher lets the children continue the work with closed eyes for a little while. They are exploring the curvature with their palms, smoothing out uneven spots by pushing and groping, which also requires the tactile sensitivity of the fingertips. Now not only the mouth is on break, but also the eyes. The majority of children can easily agree to this type of activity. After this entirely inward phase of practice, the children are asked to open their eyes again, to just put the formed clay in the palm of one hand and raise it up so that they themselves and their classmates can look and see what lovely things have been created. The teacher walks around the class, looks at the individual pieces of work, praises, admires, gives advice how to make an improvement here and there, maybe points out two or three pieces that have turned out particularly rounded and harmonious in shape. That can motivate the children to return to their own forms with loving interest, to even out any remaining uneven places.

Then the moment has arrived when each child takes his form on which he has worked for about twenty minutes and lays it against one cheek, and the other little piece of clay he had portioned off at the beginning on the other cheek. Great astonishment! How warm is the form that they worked with, how round! And how cold in contrast is the untouched piece of clay! The children report that to each other, of course, and to the teacher.

Finally each child carefully etches his or her initials with the thumbnail into the bottom of his or her form and then deposits it on the art board on the desk. Now the hands get a break! Four industrious helpers go around quietly and carefully collect the forms and position them up front on boards on the teacher's table, where they will rest under damp cloths until the next day. Careful! Beware! There are still the remaining little clay pieces on the boards in front of the children! These now need to be swiftly gathered up under strict supervision and put into the large, vacuum-locked clay container. After all, clay is not a toy but our work material that we will need again the next time. Also the wooden work boards are quickly stashed away while other helpers wipe down the tables.

In front of the blackboard there are four buckets full of water, each on a chair with a towel draped over the back of the chair. The children get in line to wash off the thin film of dry white clay from their hands. The teacher keeps an eye on all the children during this cleanup period. This is a situation similar to painting day.

It is particularly useful and fitting to follow this forming practice with a period of mental work, especially of the kind that stimulates sophisticated use of language. In the first grade, that may be an in-depth conversation about a fairy tale that was told the day before. Or, if there happens to be a writing period afterwards, one can let the children search for words with repetitive sound sequences or perhaps those that may rhyme. How richly their language now flows from its source! Also mental arithmetic practice in the form of imaginative arithmetic stories serves as a good follow-up after such intense work with their hands! After about twenty minutes of this kind of mental and language-oriented practice, the teacher still has about twenty-five minutes left for telling a fairy tale. So the main lesson can be brought full circle on such a Monday morning in a lovely atmosphere, leaving all those involved content and happy.

The next morning, after the shared rhythmic practice of singing and speaking, the teacher will review the forming activities of the previous day with the children and will also select a few of the small art objects, still covered with a damp sheen, for further contemplation. The children tend to select mostly pieces that were formed with particular care and sensitivity, at the same time an incentive for the next time.

II

Developing a Sequence of Artistically Sculpted Clay Forms with Children

Step-by-Step Guide for Grades One through Three

The form series described herein is meant to inspire teachers, possibly also therapists and parents, to take up sculptural forming with children. The forms are elementary, plastic shapes, starting with the sphere. It is not the intent to give form to *some thing*, to imitate this or that in our surroundings. Rather, the children can simply acquire a sense of form and space for sculpted shapes through this type of sculptural forming practice.

This form sequence described is not at all designed for artists. Further, it is just an example to use as a guideline, but not to be adopted like a dogma. One should always work with children based on personal experience and insight.

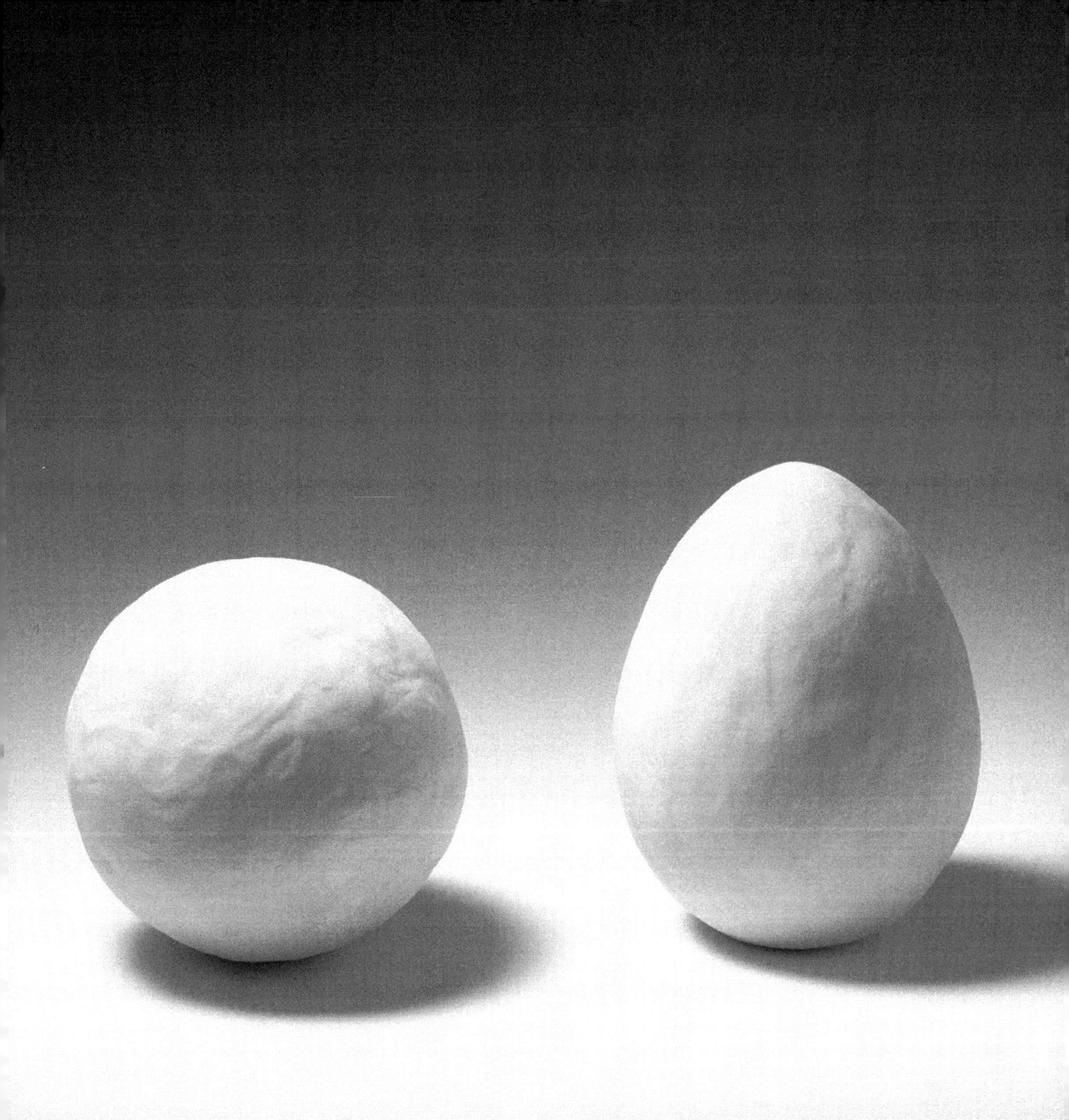

1. From a Sphere to a Three-Dimensional Oval Form

*An oval shape with one rather pointed and one rounded, blunt end emerges
as a result of the lateral squeezing of the sphere with straight, upward pointing hands while slowly,
continuously turning the form around an imaginary vertical axis.
The pressure of the hands is applied horizontally.*

After the children in the first grade have made an effort over five to six practice days to shape as evenly rounded and harmonious a form as possible, practically all of them had acquired such skill in the repetitive practice of the necessary movements that they were able to produce a centered, round shape, a sphere, in about fifteen minutes. This ball provided the basis for the first metamorphosis of form. Before beginning the next sequence of hand movements with the children, I guided them to become aware of their hands:

"Now put down your form for a moment and look at the backs of your hands. There you can see and feel the fingers emerging from the wrist like long rays, right from the hand root [the carpus area]. Your fingers are still connected in the middle hand, and then they emerge separately as your index, middle, ring and pinky fingers. That gives them the ability to move separately and freely like small limbs. If we then turn our hands around, we see how our palms show a slight inward arch, like a shallow bowl; we call this the palm or the hand-hollow. The fifth finger ray is the thumb. It emerges at the side of the middle part of the hand. It is so movable that it can meet each of the other fingers one by one. Do try it out! There, where the four finger rays emerge from the middle part of the hand [the metacarpus area], our hands are so strong that we can use them for forming in clay in a very special way. And that is what we want to try now."

The teacher underscores this introductory speech with descriptive gestures of her own hands. She has the children feel and show the respective parts of the hands as well.

"Now I take my round form between both my hands in such a way that I can squeeze it carefully with the middle part of both my hands, giving it a slight stretch upwards and downwards. In this process I slowly turn the form a little bit each time after squeezing it, always in the same direction. (For the teacher: this turning around the vertical center axis is necessary for achieving symmetry.) I squeeze and turn each time a little further, I squeeze and continue turning. Now you try it, try to stretch your own clay form, just as I have showed you."

I continue to demonstrate the movements with my form and after a while I ask for the children's attention. "If we stop now, we can see that our round shape has become slimmer and higher. If we put it upright on our palm we can now say that it has an upper and a lower end. Now we want to squeeze the upper part a bit more than the lower part. That creates a small, somewhat pointed cap at the upper end. This tip is more curved than the lower end of the form. Only straight fingers and our finger tips can help in this work."

Along with the children, I now slowly compress the upper end of the form with straight fingers more than the lower end, while turning the form slowly and continuously. Finally I put a finishing touch with my thumb on the upper end of the form where it is now more strongly curved.

Demonstration is the method! This is a process of working together, stopping, regarding, making short, guiding statements, once in awhile touching and forming with closed eyes. Then we examine our forms carefully "with the will that goes through the eye."[7] Some children notice: "But this has turned into an egg!" Yes, that is the appropriate term for the created form. The teacher can add that most eggs have one more pointed and one blunter end.

The teacher already observed during the practice that a few children squeezed the spherical form only timidly, gingerly, and achieved only a small stretch that way. When we look at our work on the next day, it is apparent that these pieces have remained still quite round. Other children may have left their forms still rather round in the lower half and too pointed in the upper part. But many children have squeezed and turned their forms so skillfully that they first stretched them equally both upwards and downwards and then could round them off at the top as appropriate for an oval. The children are aware of these variations, and they are asked to describe the shapes in a language appropriate to their age. The teacher will of course assist them as necessary and then maybe group the little sculptures accordingly.

This process in itself leads the teacher towards variation possibilities for the next rounds of practicing the oval form during the following three to four days of working with the clay.

If the entire class still should have difficulty, the teacher would be well advised to allow more practice with the children for this first transformation from sphere to oval. By repeating the movements and handgrips, the children gain increasing skill in turning their form rhythmically and evenly around an imaginary center axis, squeezing them horizontally and stretching them vertically.

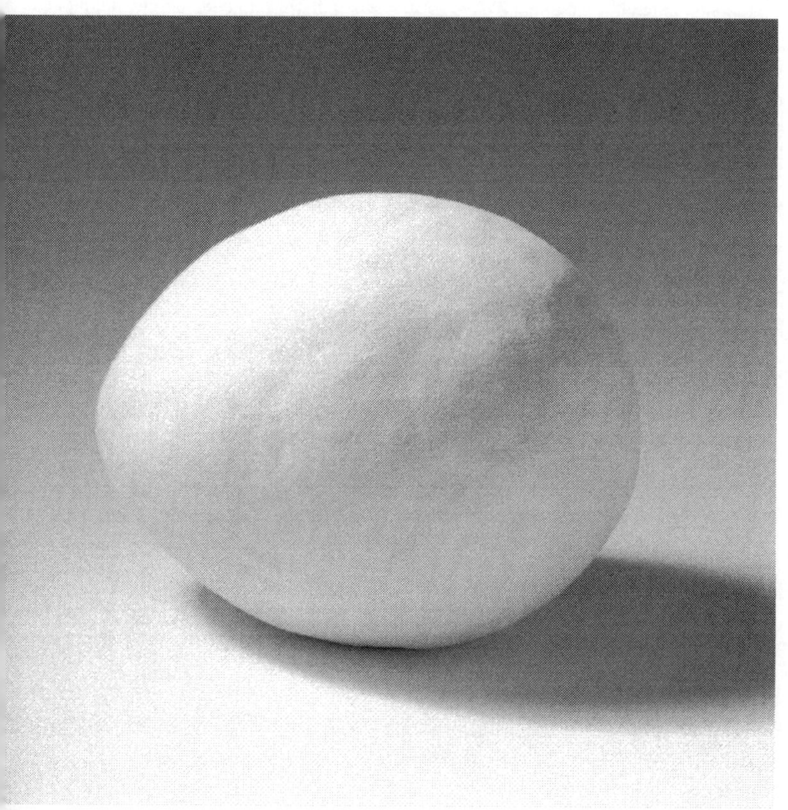

Shaped oval with one end more pointed and one blunter

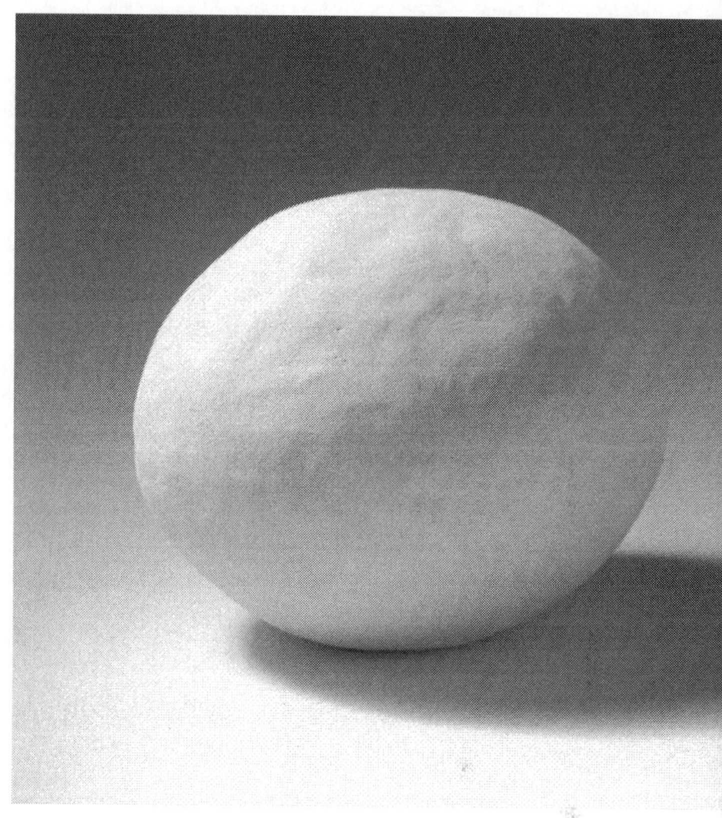

Shaped oval resting on its side with two approximately identical curved ends

Even though it is not so easy to apply more pressure to the form on the upper half than the lower half while staying aware of the symmetry of the entire form, the children can achieve it. If they sit really upright they will succeed, because a current of power flows from the spine through the shoulder blades into the shoulders and arms down to the hands to give shape to the form. "And that is the essence of artistic sensitivity, this merging with the form, this partaking in the life of the form."[8]

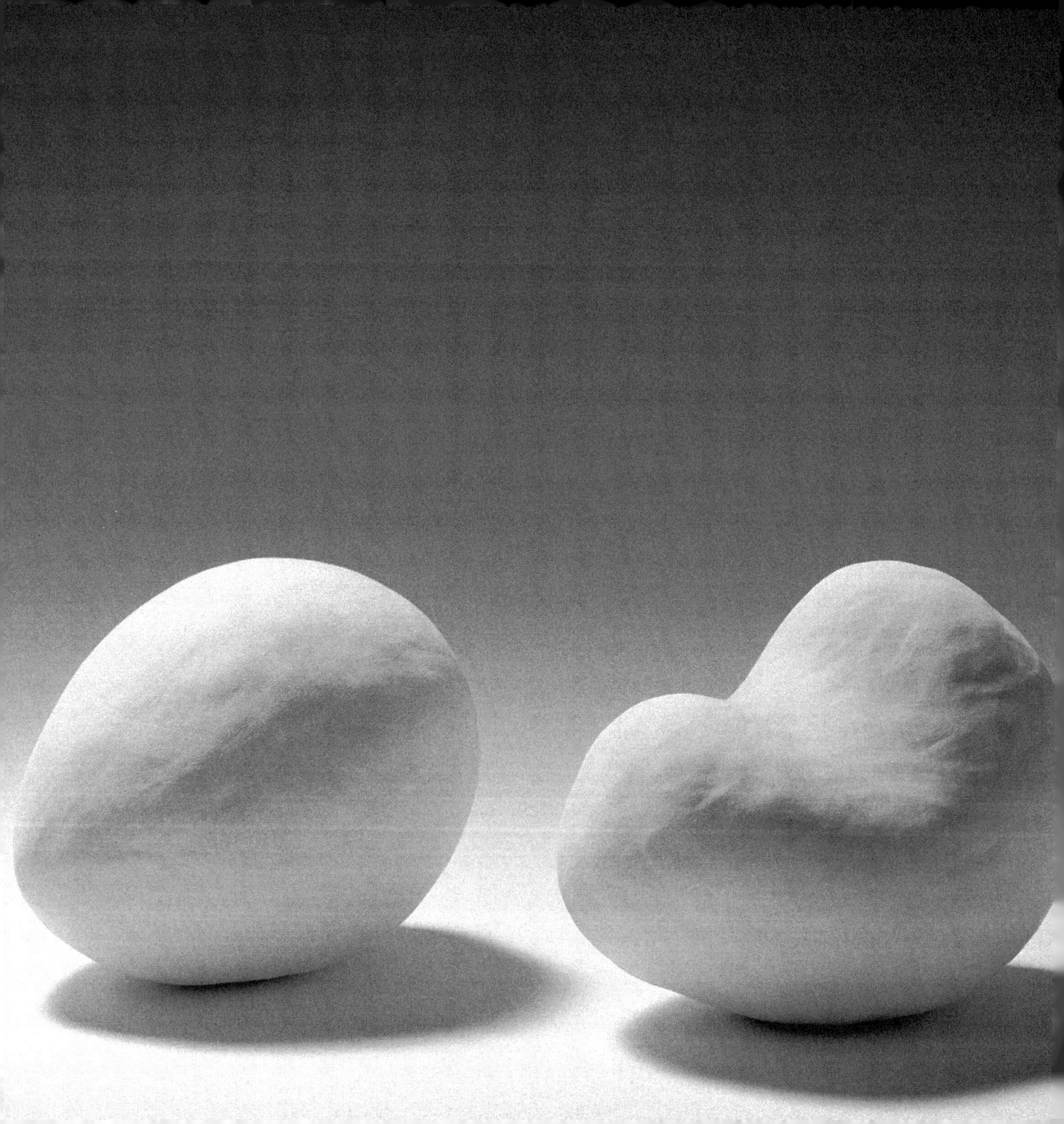

2. First Transformation of an Oval Form through Developing a Saddle Shape

This first conscious indenting of the formed clay, created by the ball of the thumb, is an elemental experience for the children. With this process they slip back into a form-gesture, which they have performed in early childhood as inner shape-givers within their own bodies. Afterwards the indent is developed into a double curved plane, a saddle plane.

After forming an oval with the children, again, I once more guide their awareness to their hands. "You now know how we can round out the clay to form a sphere. You have also learned to squeeze this sphere with the strong middle part of your hands like this, while turning it continuously in a certain direction and stretching it in the process to create a beautiful oval shape. And now we have as part of each hand this capable fellow, the thumb, who can help us do something that we haven't tried so far. Below the thumb there is this especially vigorous, somewhat rounded muscle, which we call the ball of the thumb. Check out how it feels!"

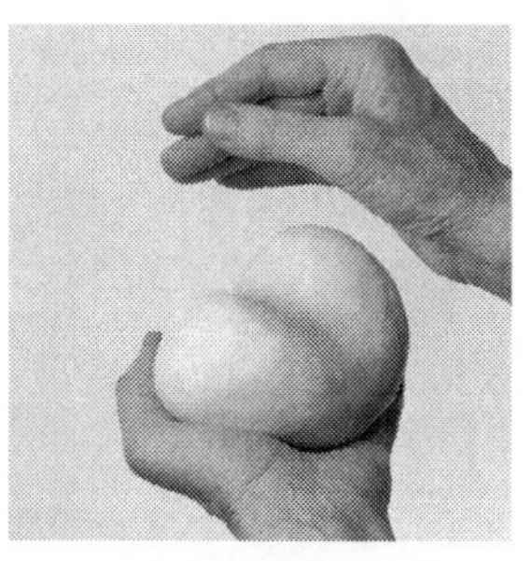

The depression is gradually added to a broader full surface.

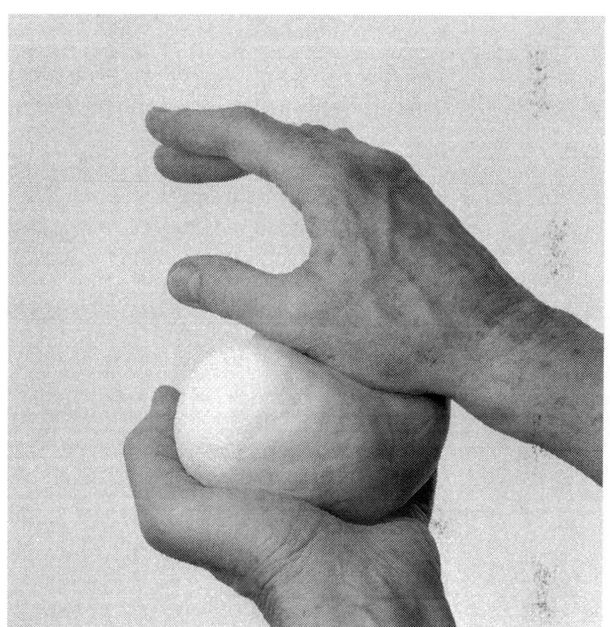

Demonstration is the method! The teacher shows the children how she indents the side of an oval clay form with the ball of her thumb.

The teacher shows the children how she indents the side of an oval clay form with the ball of her thumb.

"Now I place the oval form sideways in my left palm, and with the ball of my right thumb I press into the form, first gently then more and more firmly, to make an indent. [The ball of the thumb is best placed onto the clay at a diagonal angle; that way it quite naturally nestles into the oval form.] You are now going to do the same!" (See illustration above.)

After the children have all done this, I show them how I move the entire thumb joint back and forth in the hollow I just created. I use this rocking movement to widen the hollow so that finally a saddle plane emerges. The challenge is to create beautiful transitions between this saddle plane and the rest of the oval's curved surfaces. Again the thumb proves a suitable assistant. I have the children grasp this new form with both hands and let them gently touch all around it, so they can gain a sense for it as a whole. In this way they can even out uneven spots with the thumb and complete their form as best they can in keeping with my demonstration.

This saddle formation should be repeated two or three times, but with different oval shape variations, if possible. One time an oval shape with two equally curved ends may be the starting form, another time one with two differently curved ends.

If we now pick up the new form in both hands, we can feel how it nestles harmoniously in the hands, conveying a sense of well-being for children as well as adults.

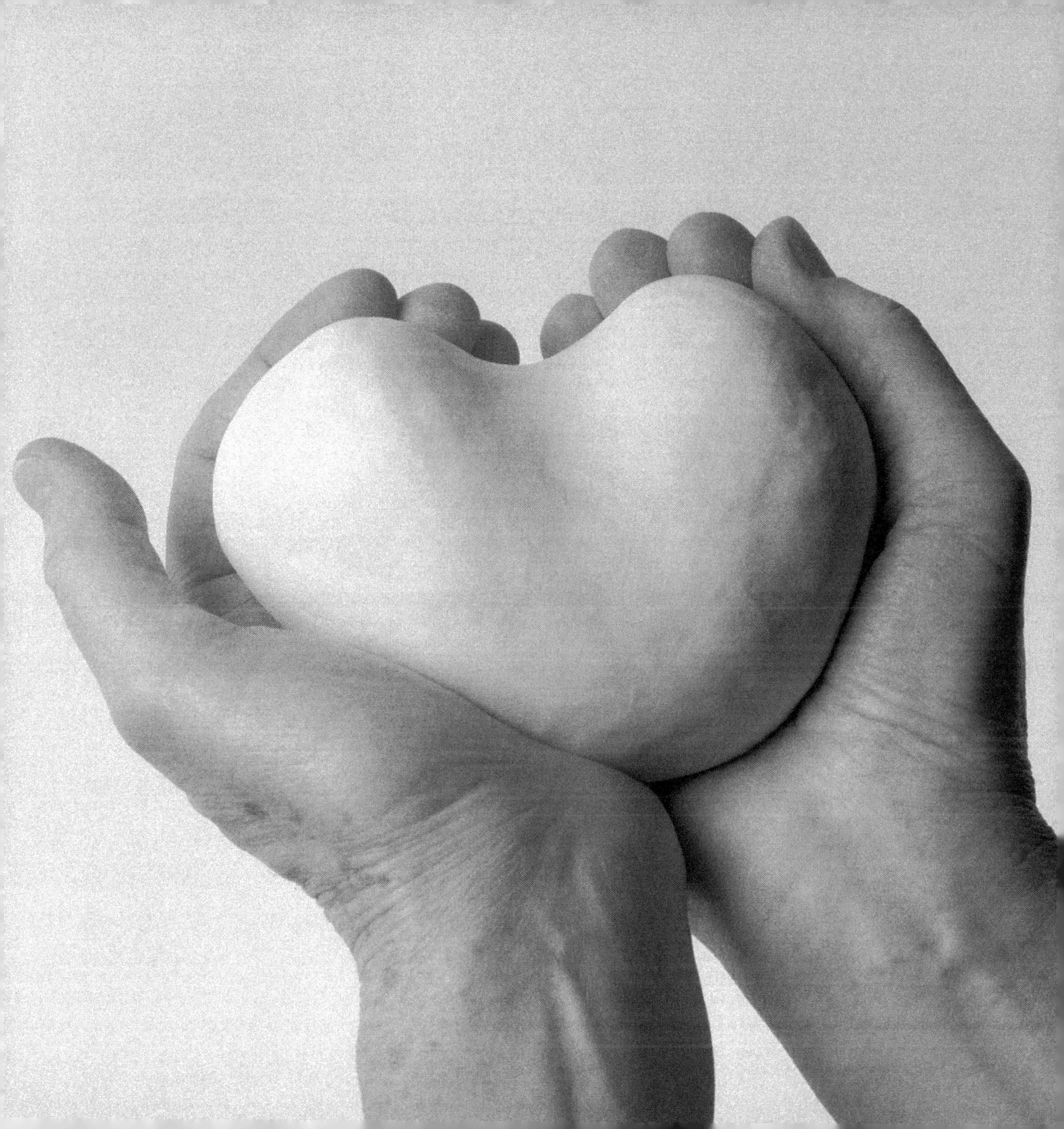

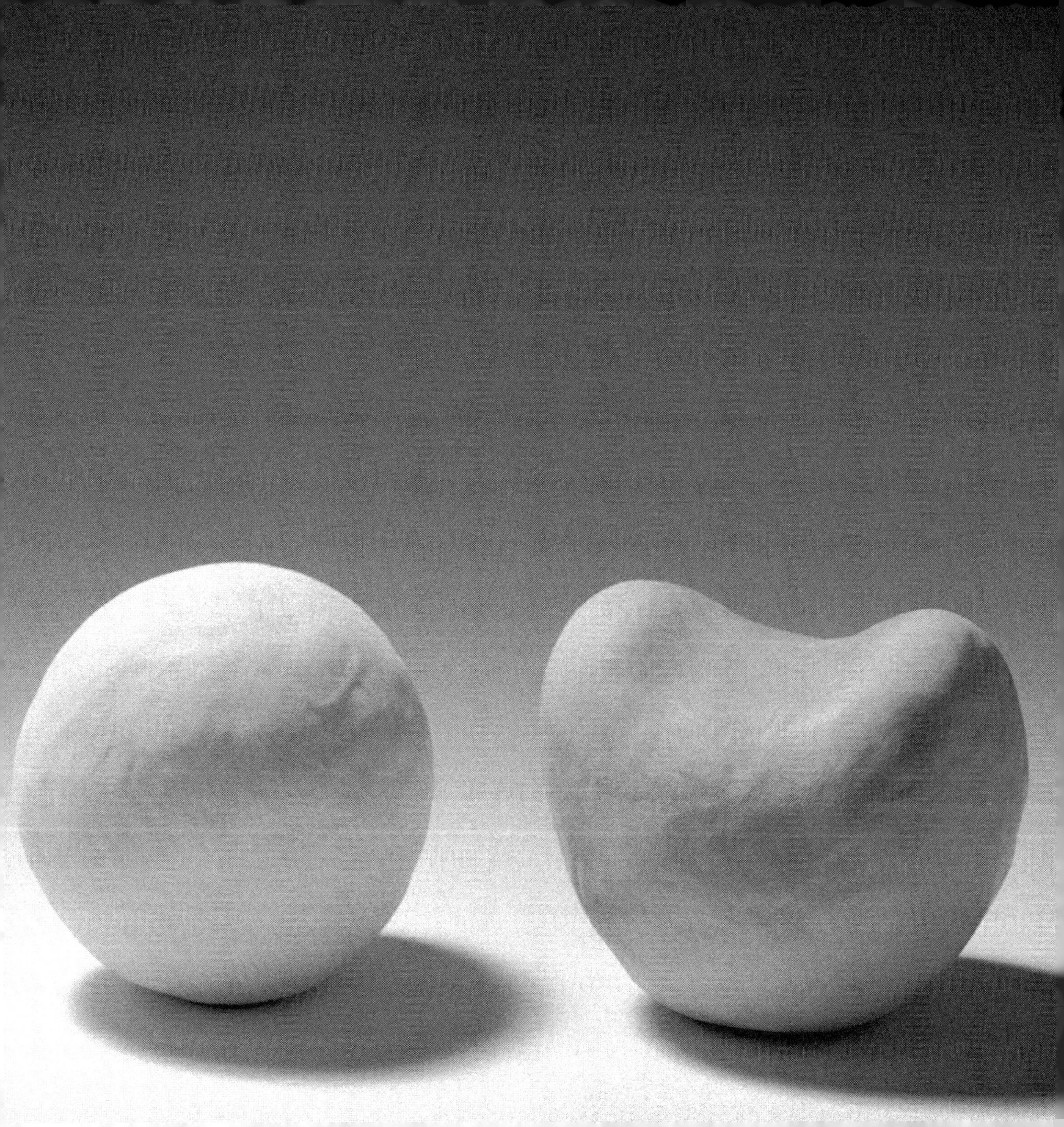

3. From a Sphere to a Three-Dimensional Right–Left Symmetry by Way of a Saddle Formation

While saddle formation in an oval, positioned on its side, could still be developed rather freely, we shall now proceed in a symmetrical way. In particular the senses of balance, touch, vision, kinesthetics, and aliveness are challenged to help achieve a harmonious right–left symmetry.

In the second grade form drawing class, the children first practice drawing shapes that are mirrored along a vertical axis: right–left symmetrical forms. The seven- to eight-year-old child will grasp the axial symmetry of a form best when it is positioned vertically just like the symmetrical axis of his own body. This shows us how closely connected the grasp of symmetry is to the awareness of one's own equilibrium.[9] I transferred this experience to the creating of a three-dimensional right–left symmetrical form with children of this age group.

The round, centered form emerged as if suspended in the balance between inside and outside, created by the rhythmical, squeezing movement of both rounded palms. The children practiced pressing a first dent and saddle formation into the sideways oval, while the parts above and below, right and left of the saddle plane had not yet been worked on in the sense of symmetry. The essential point was to experience the inward curvature of the indent and develop it into a saddle plane. The next step will require a conscious grasp of right and left in harmony with above and below.

Starting from the sphere, I guide the children as follows: "I put the round form onto my left palm. I'll call the place where it touches the hand 'below.' Now I lay the outer ridge of my right thumb on the opposite spot, which I call 'above.' Now I make a slight dent with the side of my thumb into my form, so that two identical bulges occur, one right and one left of the indent. I widen the indent with my thumb ball and thumb, again using the rocking motion we practiced before. Now you will do the same!"

The children need to be encouraged with various hand movements to explore, through touch and sensing, the right–left symmetry created here by the saddle formation to finally get a balanced form. It is helpful to hold the form after a while in both hands so that the bent fingers nestle around the sides and into top of the saddle shape, but be careful not to claw! Now the child can even out any uneven spots, acting always from inner balance.

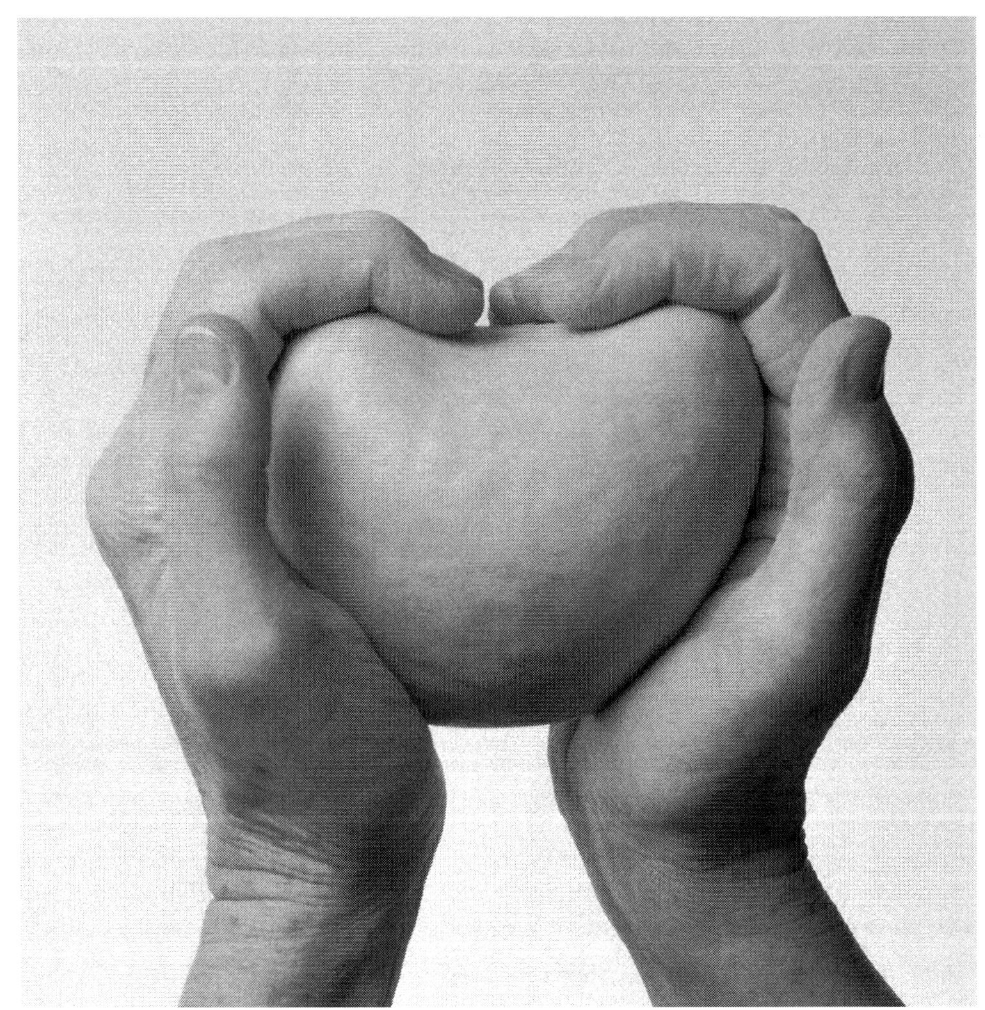

When the form is held with both hands so that the fingers nestle into the saddle plane, the fingertips can even out any bumps and explore by touch to achieve a truly symmetrical form.

Afterwards we turn the form 180 degrees around the vertical axis so that the saddle plane can be viewed from the back side. It is best to repeat this several times. It will help the children to muster the patience necessary and to ever again use their visual assessment faculties to shape a truly symmetrical form. The point here is also to create beautiful transitions between the inward curve of the saddle plane and the bulge of the outer planes. There should be no sharp edges.

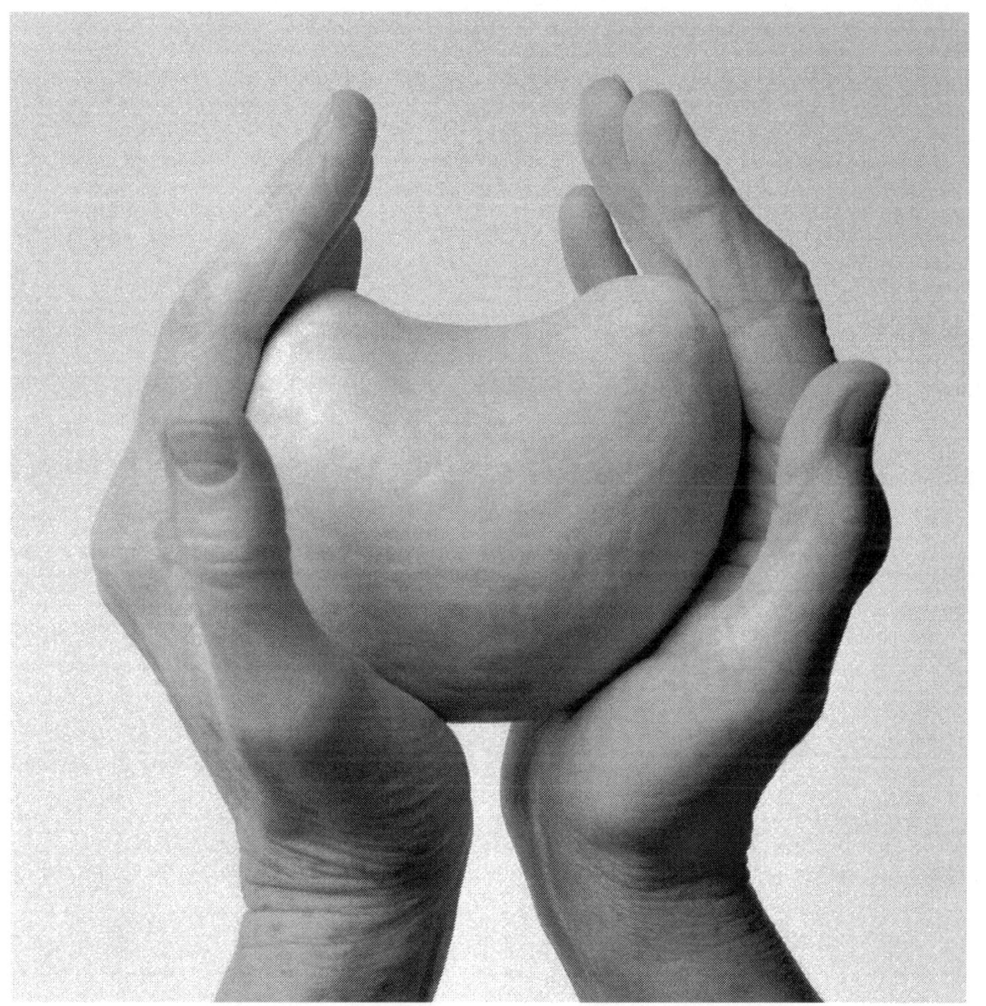

Here the feeling hands cradle a view of a saddle plane with two symmetrical mounds right and left. With this gesture, the teacher now guides the children towards checking their right–left symmetry. The children "explore the forms with the eye and [also] with the will going through the eye."[10]

Towards the end of this forming process, I have the children position their forms upside down in their hands, so that the upper, sculpted part touches the palm. Then they can feel with the other hand that the lower part of the form has kept its curvature intact and that so far there has been only a shape change in the upper half.

This symmetrical form should also be practiced several times. It helps to have the children first press a relatively small saddle plane into the clay sphere, because it does not so drastically change the roundness of the form, making it easier to achieve a right–left symmetry. In repeat practice sessions they can be guided to widen the saddle plane and to take good notice of the changes that occur to the right and left sides of the sphere. So I give a new focus to each practice session. One time I emphasize keeping the form nice and full, so it does not become scraggly and skinny. Another time I may suggest that the form surface should get a fine finish.

With such guidance, the children become gradually more and more skillful and independent in their handling of the clay. It helps them to consciously master this first regular organization of the spherical form.

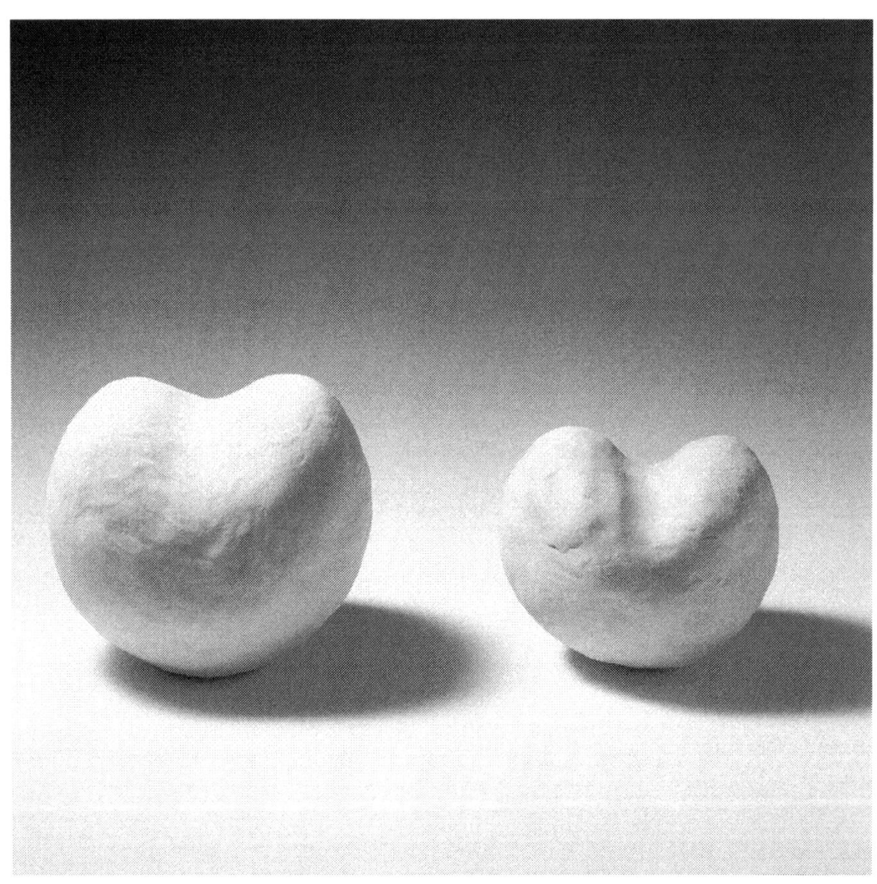

Right–left symmetry form with a relatively small saddle plane; on the right, the form of an eight-year-old girl in the second grade, on the left, the teacher's form

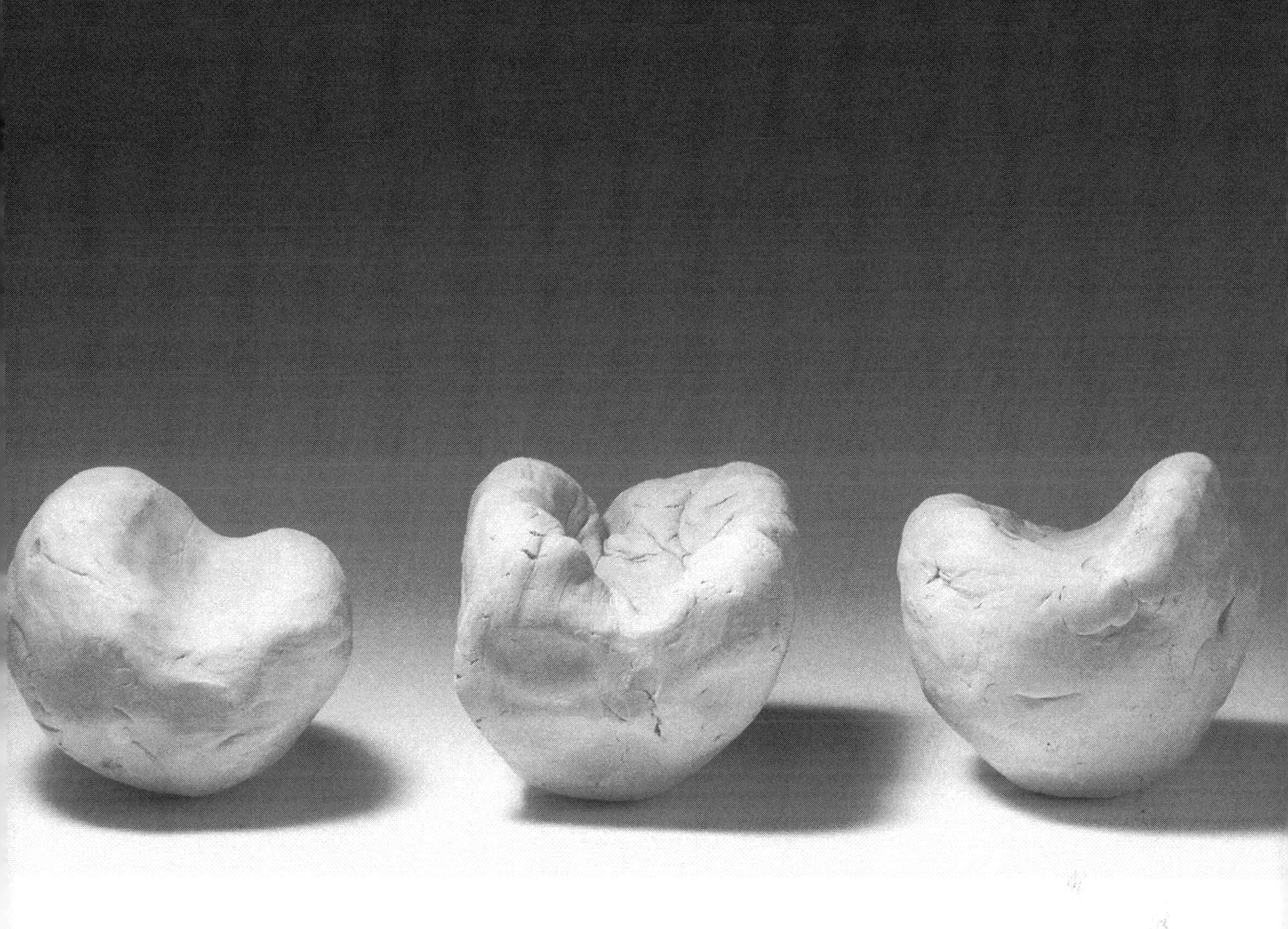

Following the same instructions, three second-graders created these right–left symmetrical forms.
It is apparent that it is not at all easy – in spite of sincere efforts – to create beautiful forms

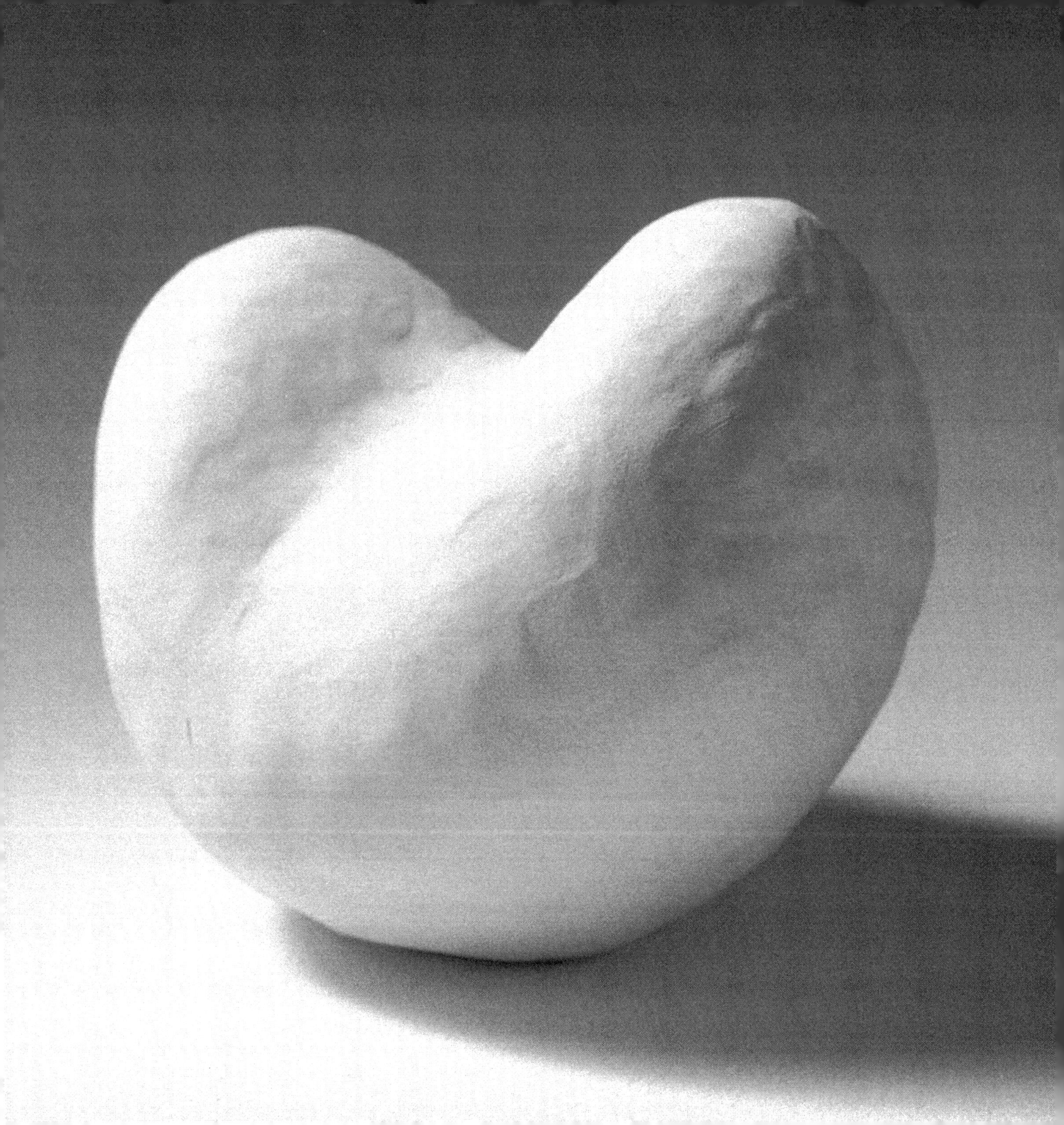

4. Transforming Right–Left Symmetry into an Asymmetrical Form

Now right–left symmetry, which had been consciously formed, is changed into an asymmetrical shape. One side is "awakened" by the shaping hands while the other side is still "dreaming." The children thus experience that the language of form is diverse and alive.

The children are now prepared to immerse themselves enthusiastically in a lively transformation of the right–left symmetry. The same shape is formed once more, just like before. Then I can suggest to the children, "You now have given a thorough structure to the upper part of your form, giving it a right side and a left side. But it seems as if it were asleep. My form too seems to be still asleep. Now I want to wake it up with my warm hands. Look how I do that! Is there already something stirring in the center? One side grows and stretches, wants to extend upwards, out of the roundness. With my hollow hand I help it along, and move carefully some of the clay upwards from the bottom part, which is still unchanged. That way, the outer shape can retain its roundness. So far, the other side of the top part has only been dreaming, but now it too awakens, and gradually stretches a little bit. How amazed this side is to see its counterpart has grown so much! Does it also want to grow so tall? No, it would rather wait and rest a little while, and I let it do that. Now you also wake up your forms!"

A little later then: "Now our hands explore gently along the path between the larger and the smaller mounds and try to form a beautiful, smooth transition between them. We also want to create a nice a transition from the lower part of our form to the upper part."

It remains important to keep the children's forming activities continuously guided by the way I handle the clay, not only during the initial introduction to the new task.

Two student forms from the second grade: these two small sculptures show that the children were inspired by the teacher's suggestions and followed them in their sculpting process. But you can also see how difficult it was for them at first to work out smooth transitions between the saddle areas on one side and the mounds on the other.

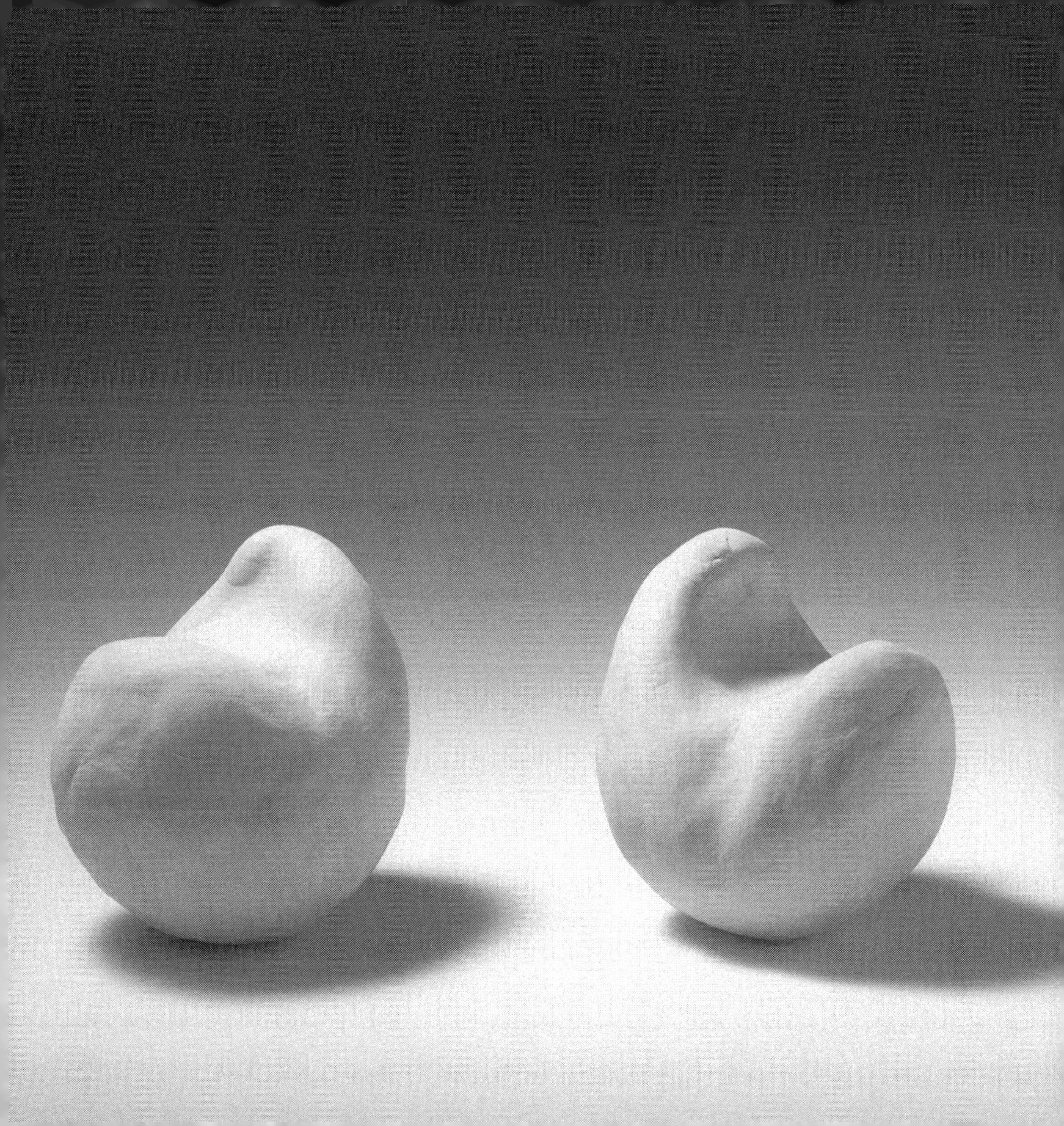

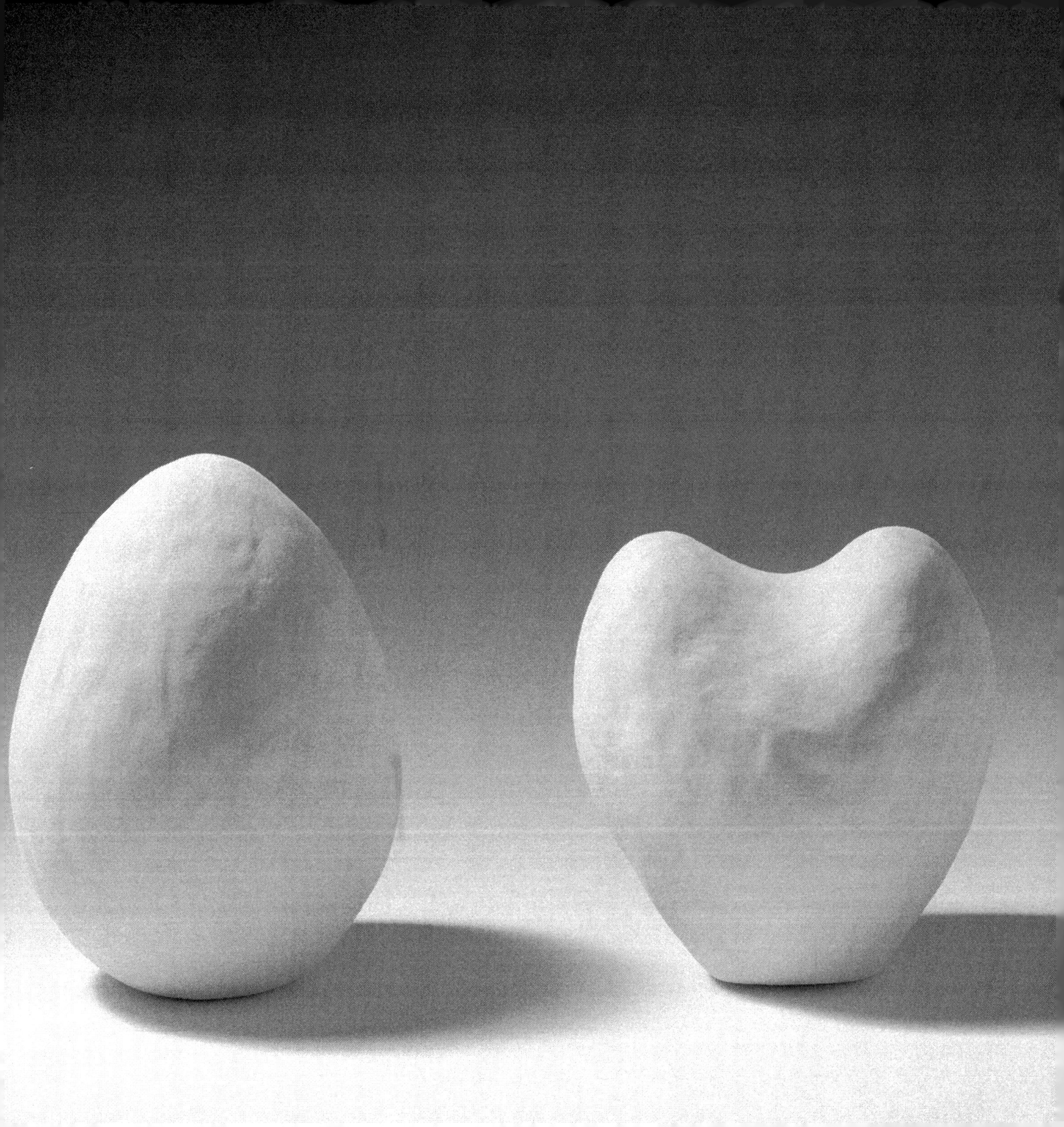

5. From an Oval Shape to a Right–Left Symmetrical Form

How much easier and how much more graceful this right–left symmetrical form looks compared with the one that was shaped from a sphere. Why is that so?

After the previous exercises only few words of guidance are necessary for creating this form. We accompany the children again in their process of transforming a sphere into an oval shape. Then we ask them to position the oval vertically on the left palm, if possible in such a way that the more curved end is pointing upwards. Then we encourage the children to make an imprint in the middle of this upper part with the ball of their thumb. From there we keep working just like in the first right–left symmetry exercise in which we had started with the shape of a sphere. It is important during this process to form both of the now emerging mounds in a well-balanced, symmetrical way, so that they are evenly rounded and equally high. Between the mounds and the saddle plane in the center as well as the outer curved planes, the transitions should be fashioned to appear smooth, "gliding" and gentle. Finally the form is positioned on the board with slight pressure, so it will not topple over. The children have to be careful to make sure their forms stand really upright for in this position the right–left symmetry to find its best expression.

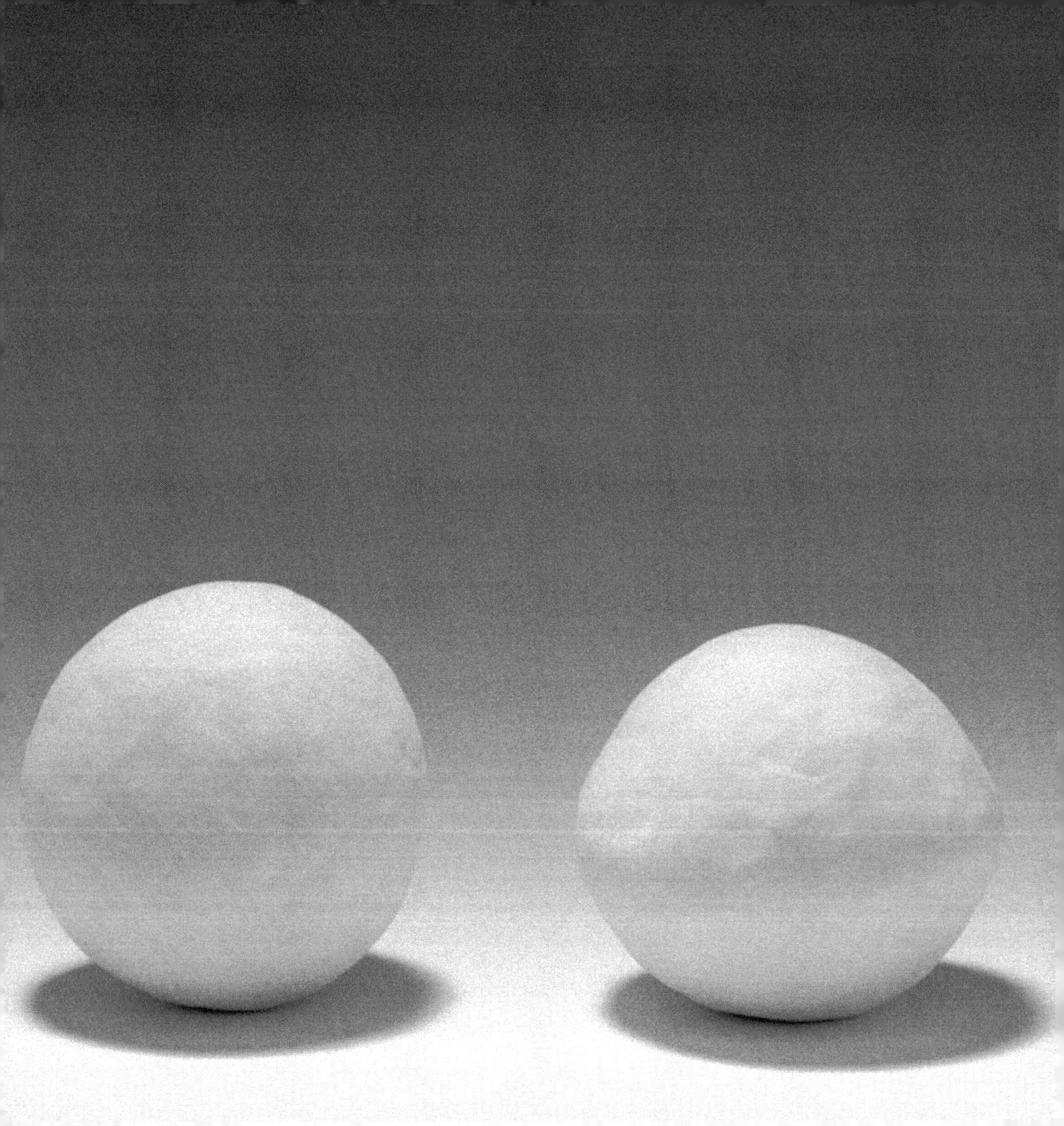

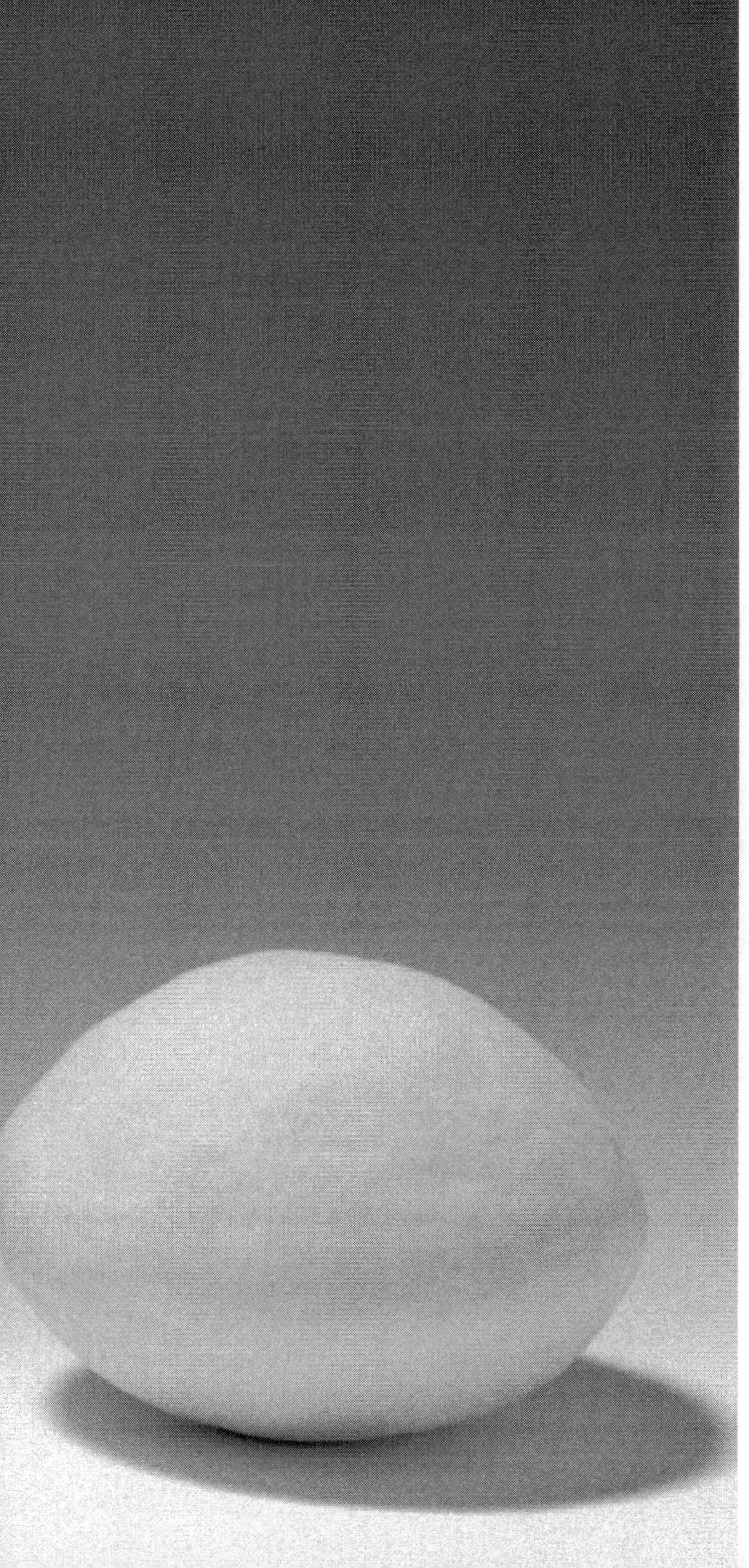

6. From a Sphere to a Flattened Sphere

The challenge is to flatten a sphere in such a way that top and bottom parts still retain a certain roundness. We use an imaginary horizontal middle plane as an orientation to arrive at a balanced symmetrical form – a symmetrical mirror image with upper and lower curvature. Here the curved planes must be formed with particular visual and tactile awareness. Pushing and turning now bring about a flattening and not an elongation like in the oval.

In the first transformation of the sphere, the children learned to elongate the round form vertically, towards an upper and a lower direction, creating a three dimensional oval shape. Then, in a further step, they practiced making a first indent into the resting oval, forming a saddle plane. After that, shapes followed that started with the sphere and allowed the children to discover and practice tactile exploration of a three dimensional right–left symmetry.

During second grade, eight-year-olds are taught to first practice the right–left symmetry in form drawing before proceeding to mirror image forms with a horizontal axis. This also works for sculptural forming. However, this step from right–left symmetry to an upper–lower mirroring process in this three-dimensional space of form is a completely different experience than that of drawing such mirror images in a two-dimensional plane. In the following I describe an approach that a teacher can take with the children when modeling in this direction.

We begin again with a sphere, and then the children are guided as follows, "Now I put the sphere onto my left palm. The left hand now supports and holds it, while my right hand gently and evenly pushes down from above. Now I turn the form a little further around its vertical axis and again gently push down from above. Now I turn the form so that the part of the sphere that lay in my palm now faces upwards. Again I push down gently, turn it a little and once more push carefully down from above. Do try yourself now what I just showed you!" The children and I work simultaneously, each on our own form. Several times we repeat the process of gently pushing and rotating while frequently turning over the forms in our left hand to assure their symmetry. After a period of practicing, I say, "If we now look at our forms, we see that they appear slightly flattened on both sides. I wonder if we were able to make the upper and the lower parts match. We evaluate the symmetry with our eyes, by putting our forms onto the flat left palm and stretching out our arms.

But since I do not want to flatten the form any further and retain a certain curvature, I guide the children as follows: "My form now rests on my left hand. Now I grasp the upper, slightly flattened half of the sphere with my whole right hand. I make sure that the fingers are closing tightly, without space in between. So now I push and at the same time round out the upper part of the sphere." It is a kind of "sucking grip" with the hollow of my palm. Little by little I keep turning the form on its vertical axis until it has completed one full turn, squeezing and rounding it all the while to make sure it is really even all around. After that I turn the form over in my left hand and do the same with the lower part. "You can all do the same thing now, and you can always look up and watch how I am doing it." This process is repeated several times, depending on how well the forming process is going, while working as rhythmically and evenly as possible.

Then we need to check again if the upper and the lower flattened parts of the sphere are approximately equal in curvature and size all around, that is, if they mirror each other along an imaginary horizontal middle plane. To compensate for disproportions that often appear now around the rim of the horizontal center plane, so-to-speak at the equator of the form, we continue as follows:

"Now I take the flattened sphere between both my hands extended vertically – like this – so that the flatter parts of the sphere are nestled snug in my hollow hands. My fingertips meet up here and the bottom parts of my hands touch down there. As I keep turning the form now slowly, little by little [around an imaginary vertical center plane], I feel with my fingertips that I have really vigorously squeezed the formerly round globe there, where now the two flattened halves of the sphere meet." [The normal slight curvature of the sphere has taken on a significantly stronger bent.]

"Now I try to make this special outer area particularly beautiful and even by exploring the form with my fingertips, pushing a bit where necessary and evening it out, then turning it a little further. Now you do it just like that!" This is an entirely new challenge and experience for the children, allowing them to further develop and fine-tune their spatial form awareness.

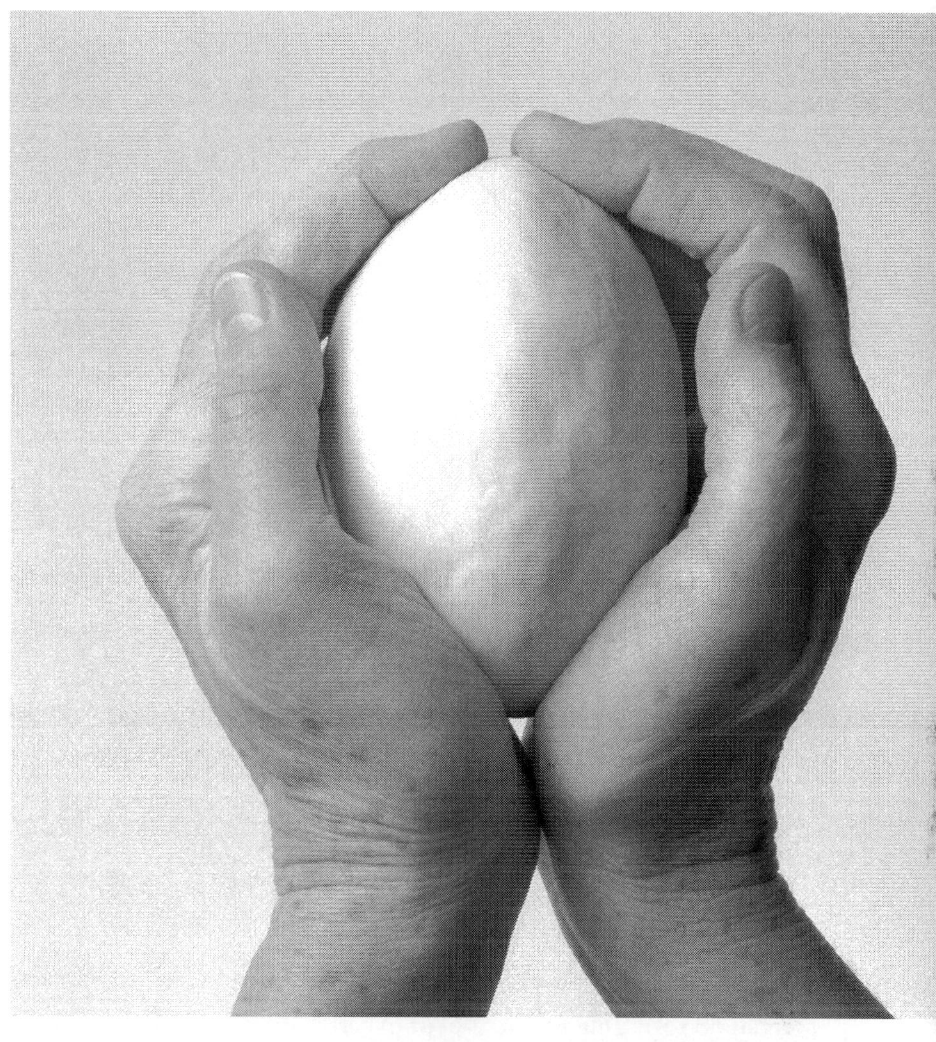

This hand position allows our fingertips to rather evenly level out the areas of greatest curvature all around the form – while our work is always centered in the inner sense of equilibrium and balance.

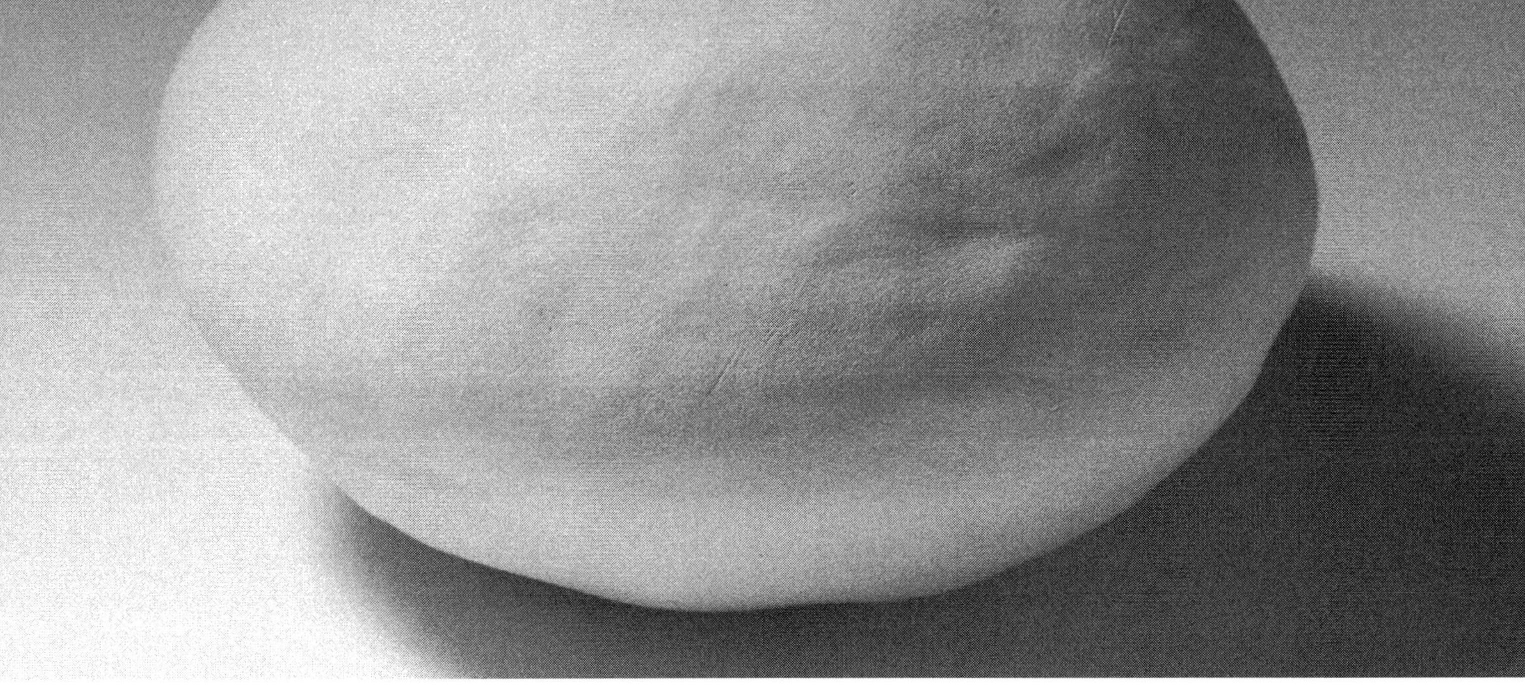

It is helpful to check again after a few minutes to be sure that the form is symmetrical. To do this I put it again on my outstretched left hand and examine it visually to see if the strongly curved rim is even all around. This task is not easy for the children, and yet I find it important to practice it with them, keeping in mind once more Steiner's recommendation regarding the first school years: "Evoke in the child a sense for the difference between the circle curvature and the elliptical curvature. In short, awaken the form-sense before the urge to imitate is awakened!"[11]

After a few exercises in second grade, one can actually let this form rest and resume the process in third grade. The children will be glad, when, then with heightened form and space-awareness, they can create perhaps even more beautiful forms than they could have earlier.

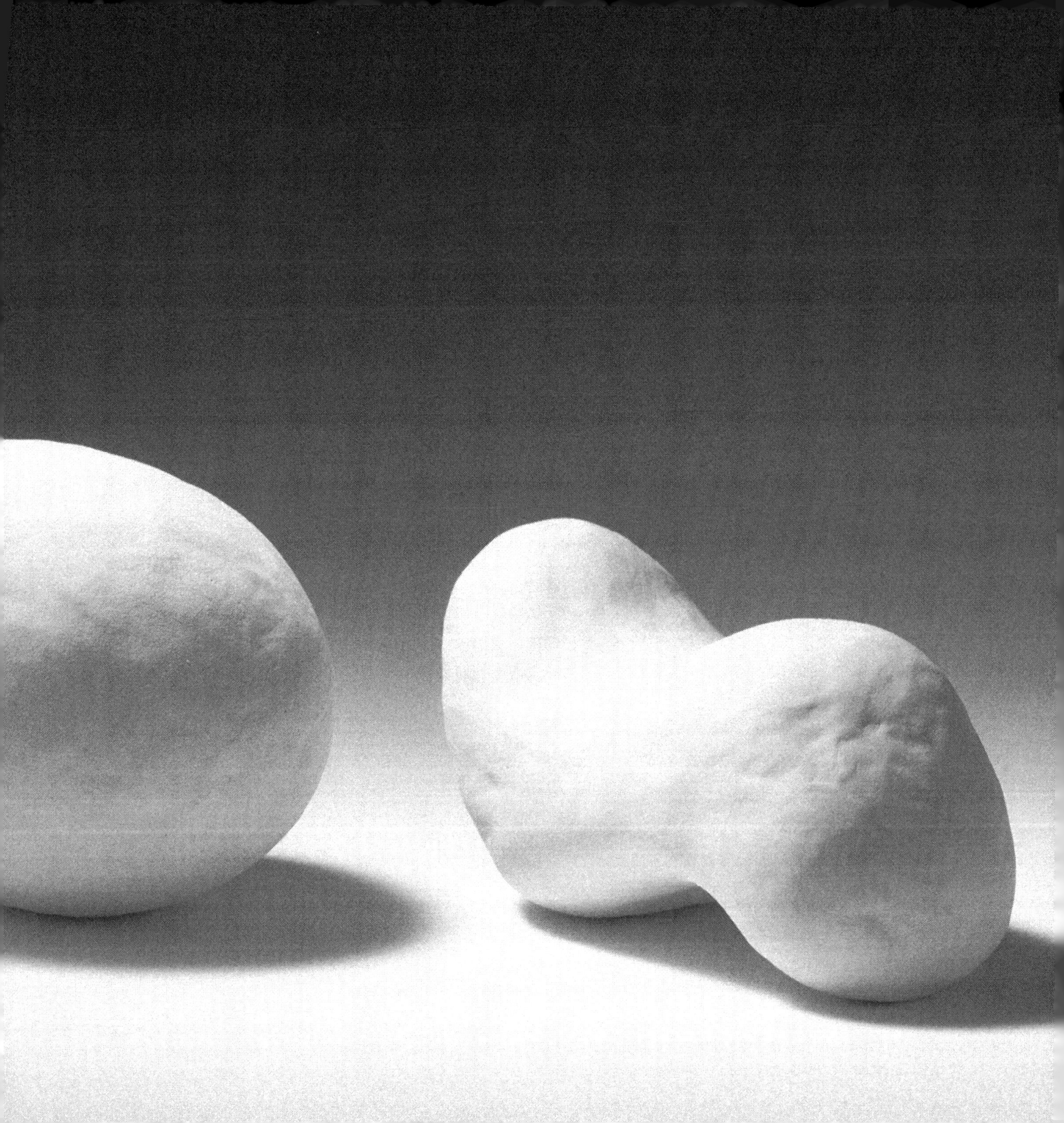

7. From a Three-Dimensional Oval to a Form with Two Saddle Planes

A new challenge: Both saddle planes should be in harmony, but not symmetrical as in the previous task. The child should try to form a beautiful, harmoniously-proportioned sculpture based on his or her form-sense and form-awareness.

Hopefully class teachers have experienced that artistically creative exercises with children at school are most successful if they themselves actively immerse themselves in working with form, color, and motif during the evening prior to the respective class. This is true for all art forms, whether it be form drawing, painting with watercolors, drawing with wax crayons, or working in clay. This prior active engagement of the teacher with the artistic medium and theme generates experiences which gestate during the night's sleep. That is how one gains the certainty necessary for the creative hand gestures and the appropriate choice of words to inspire the children to engage in artistic activities. This type of experience can also be helpful for the next form transformation.

Starting with a spherical shape, we first sculpt an oval, swiftly and paying particular attention to creating the form. Finishing the surface is of secondary importance because it will be changed later anyway. I lay the oval sideways onto my left hand and push an indent into the right half of the shape, using the thumb and ball of the thumb of my right hand. Then I broaden the indent into a saddle plane, a process that I have practiced with the children already (see No. 2 of the form sequence). Now I turn the form in my palm at a 180-degree angle so that this saddle plane now faces downwards. Then I press another indent into the left half of the side of the oval shape that is now faced upwards, again using my thumb and the ball of my thumb, and then broaden that into a saddle plane. When I look at the form now, when I turn it and view it again, it seems crude.

Next, we are challenged to beautify the two saddle planes with form-awareness and good visual judgment. We shape the form, alternately attending to the upper, then the lower saddle plane, trying to achieve a harmonic proportion, not necessarily symmetrical.

If necessary, we can deepen the saddles and/or make them wider, staying attentive to the beautiful transitions between the concave planes and the convex bulges. This newly emerging form now has planes with multiple curvatures which require sensitive tactile exploration and subtle sensory immersion. In working with this shape, it is particularly important to repeatedly encourage the children to close their eyes and touch the form, so that they again and again get a feeling for the form as a whole and assess if the indents, the mounds, and the transitions are beautifully formed, nestling snug in the hands. After continuing to work for a while, we put the form onto our outstretched hand and look appraisingly at our own forms and those of our neighbors. We may discover together how to further improve the shapes and make them even more beautiful. In a few minutes we will then finish the work. From experience, the children already know that the second attempt will be more successful!

If time permits, we can use another quarter hour at the beginning of the next morning to further improve the unfinished forms. If I decide to take that step, I ask the children while I demonstrate to carefully wrap their forms in a thin, damp (not wet!) cotton cloth, then plastic wrap, and mark them with name tags.

Steiner taught us that the etheric body is active during the night. "Due to its inherent vibratory power the etheric- or image-forming body always tends to perfect and expand that which we present to it. We just have to give this etheric- or image-forming body the appropriate opportunity to further perfect those things which we instill in it."[12] "If we prepare the etheric- or image-forming body during waking hours to not only keep resonating during sleep, but also review daytime experiences, then the child can gain insight into asymmetrical symmetries through these vibrations. The child awakens in the morning in a body of formative forces, which is internally and organically full of movement, with a likewise affected physical body. That imbues the human being with a tremendous vital force."[13] We can experience again and again that the forms we practiced in form drawing during the day are completed and harmonized within us, and within the children, during the night, enabling us to form even more beautiful and perfect shapes on the next day.

That is certainly also true for modeling. The next morning, the children will enjoy the task of further refining their forms and it does not take much time from the rest of the main lesson!

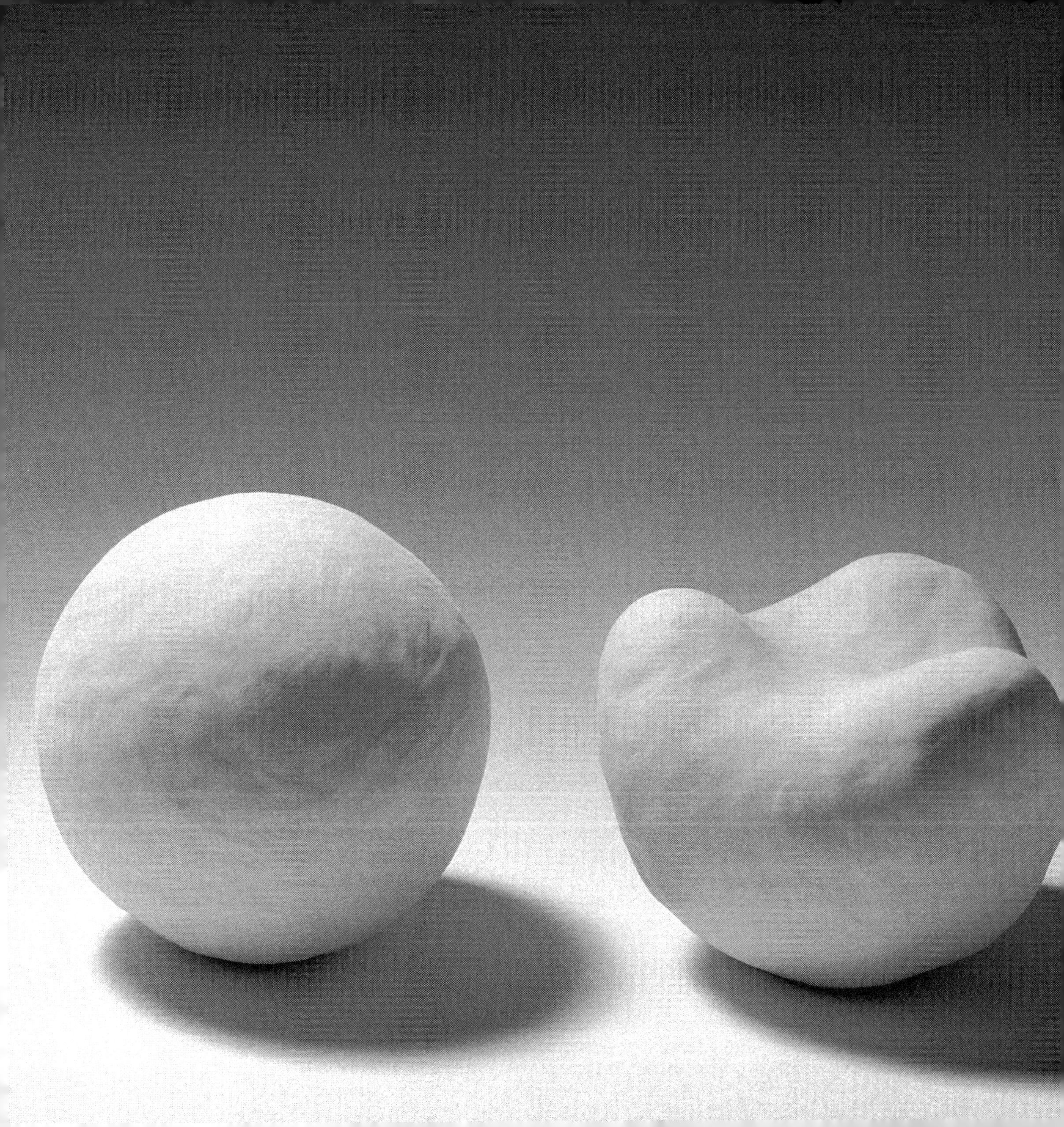

8. From a Sphere to a Threefold Symmetrical Form

As we gradually form three small hollows in the upper part of the sphere and widen them three evenly rounded mounds take shape. Three even saddle planes are formed, and in the center a shallow depression. We form the transitions between these elements with tactile sensitivity and skillful thumb movements, gradually achieving a harmonic threefold structure, which again serves as the basis for many further transmutations of form.

Again we begin with a sphere. The children place their forms on their wooden boards and I guide them by saying, "Today you have to be particularly attentive to let your eyes read my hands as they are showing you what to do! I take the rounded form into both my hands like this, so that both my thumbs rest side by side on the top. In this position, I push the clay firmly with the front parts of my thumbs. Now I move my hand hollows a little bit away from the form, but my fingers keep holding it. I open my thumbs, which are still on top so that they can form the capital letter 'A.' The tips of my thumbs keep touching, and the rest of my thumbs forms the two parts. Now I will imprint the 'A' into the clay. Try now to do the same, while I repeat the hand movements together with you." The result of these efforts is a bulge and two valleys, with some clay oozing out at the outer rim. These markers shall help to shape an even threefold structure in the top part of the form (I strive towards a threefold symmetry).

I continue to talk to the children: "You see, in this spot it pushes and moves upwards, the clay bulges and grows out of the round shape. But here, on the other side, it still rests, it still sleeps. That is the place I now indent a little with my thumb. Look, to the right and left side of it, there is an urging from inside out; the clay pushes upwards. It can be formed and rounded by our hands. My thumb senses and explores what has bulged upwards from the darkness to the light, and I can even out the resulting three small bulges with my thumb."

Now my hands hollow the form sideways. I position both thumbs and a middle finger into each of the valleys between the bulges respectively. While turning the form slowly around the vertical axis in one direction, I place the three fingers again and again into the three indents while shaping and leveling it.

Then I move my thumb sensitively across the bulges, here and there pushing a little clay upwards from the outside of the form to plump out the bulges.

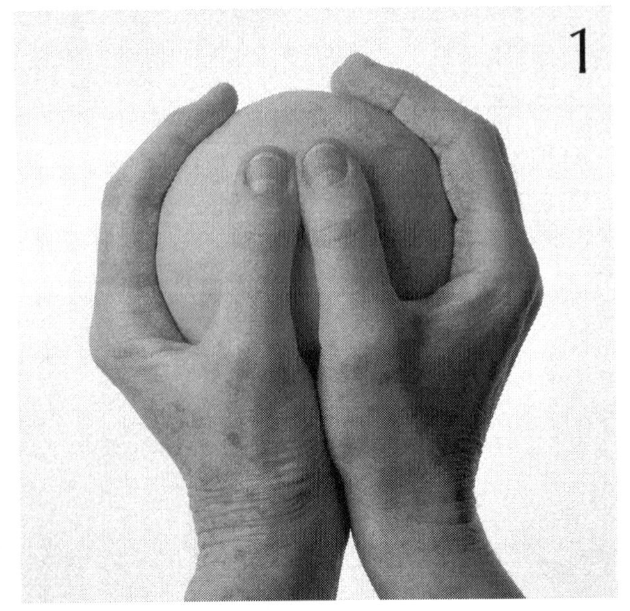

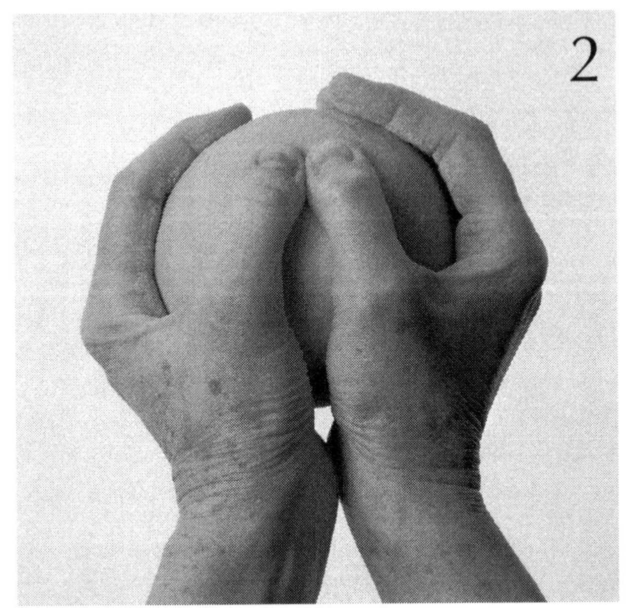

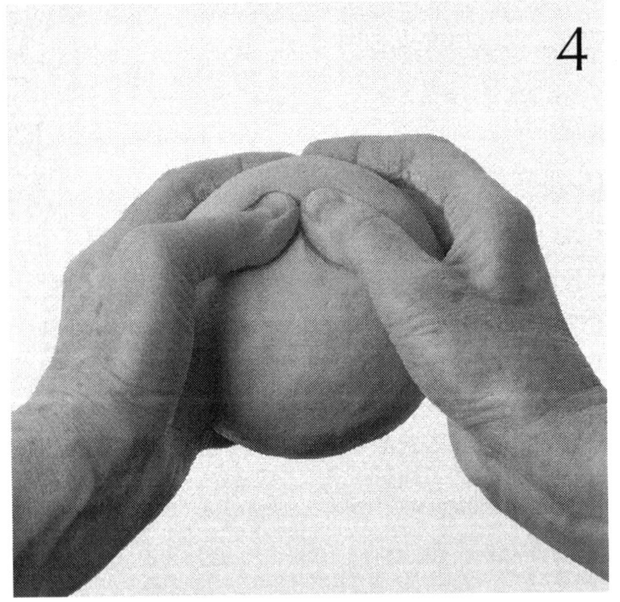

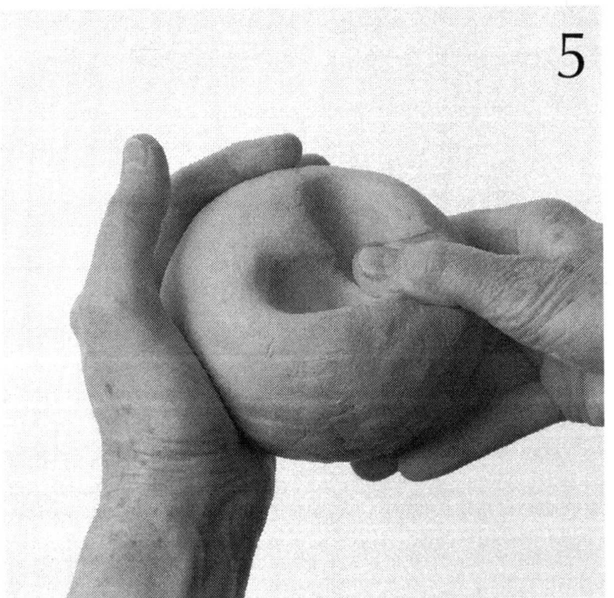

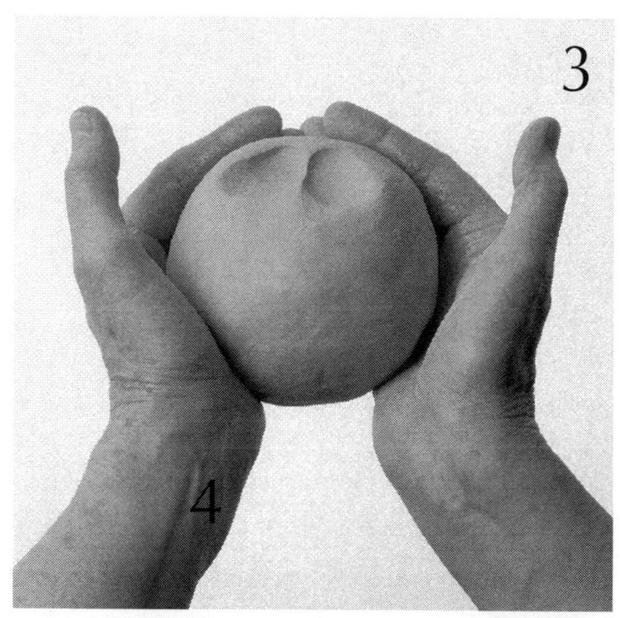

Left: *Six steps illustrating the formative process of the threefold symmetry form*

Bottom right: *Grip for finishing the form*

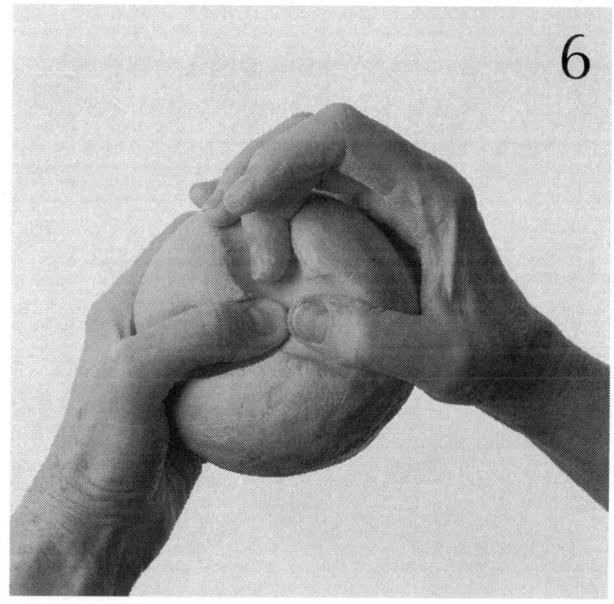

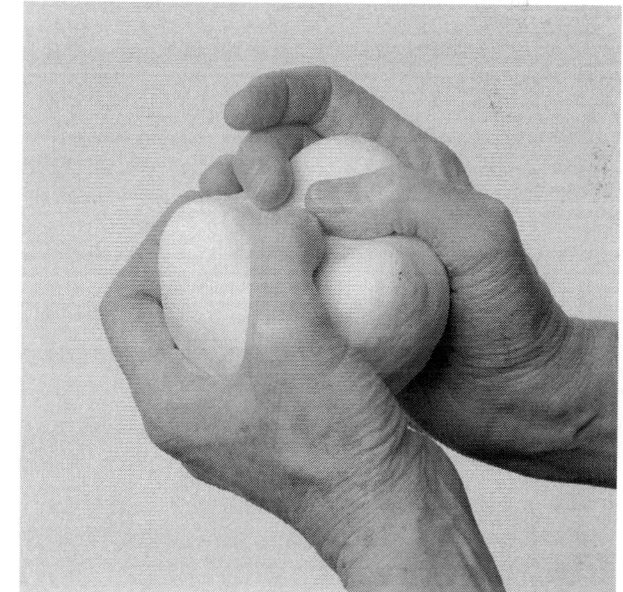

"I move my thumb across and in between the mounds and into the softly indented hollow in the center, back and forth. My thumbs carefully even out the paths; the entire form gains ever more life and beauty."

After working together this way for a while, we cup the form with both hands and turn it slowly on the vertical center axis. At the same time we carefully compress the upper half of the form a little bit, turn it and repeat the process. [The pressure is applied horizontally!] This is to help us keep the three mounds in proximity to each other, to not bulge out too broadly. If we now position the clay form upside down on one hand, we see that it has remained round at the bottom; we only transformed the upper half into a threefold form. Afterwards we still have to check and explore the transition between the upper and lower half and have to even out any small dents, tears, and bulges. Finally, the thumb explores once more across the entire form and gives it the finishing touch. For this task I needed about thirty, at most thirty-five minutes of actual modeling time with my class. Then it is cleanup and tidying.

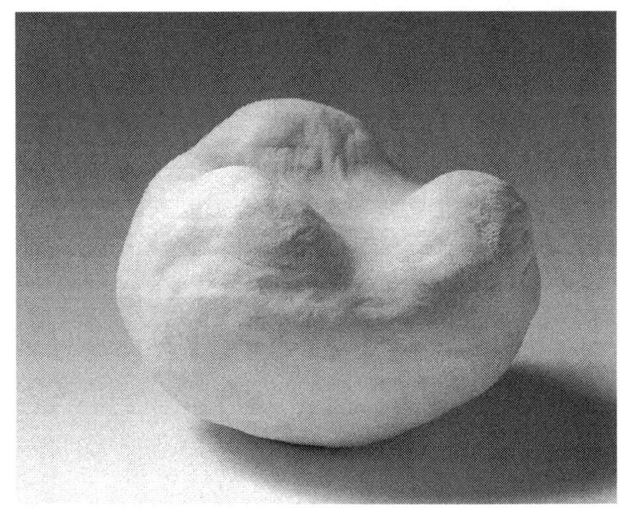

Threefold symmetrical form sculpted by a nine-year-old boy in the third grade

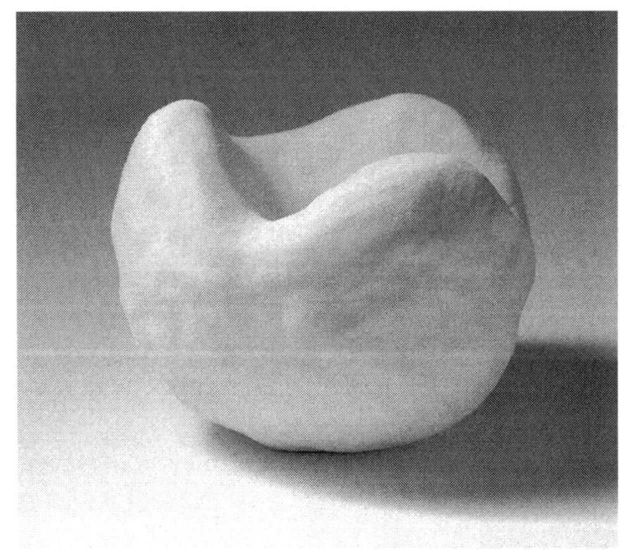

Threefold symmetrical form by a nine-and-a-half-year-old girl. This artistically gifted and behaviorally precocious child has worked out a fairly deep hollow into her otherwise very harmonious sculpture.

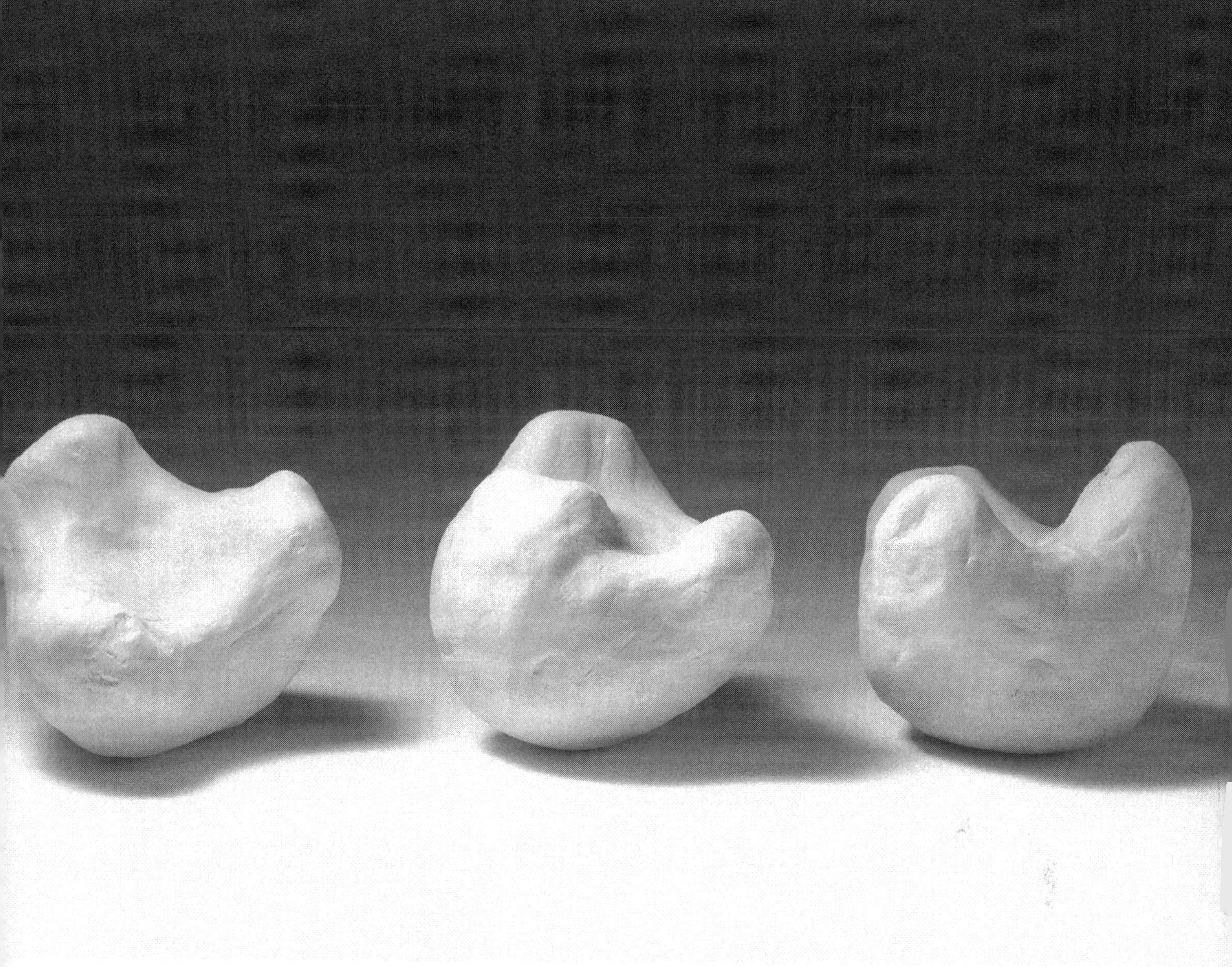

These forms were created by third graders under the same conditions as those shown on the pictures to the left. A comparison shows how difficult it is to create a balanced form.

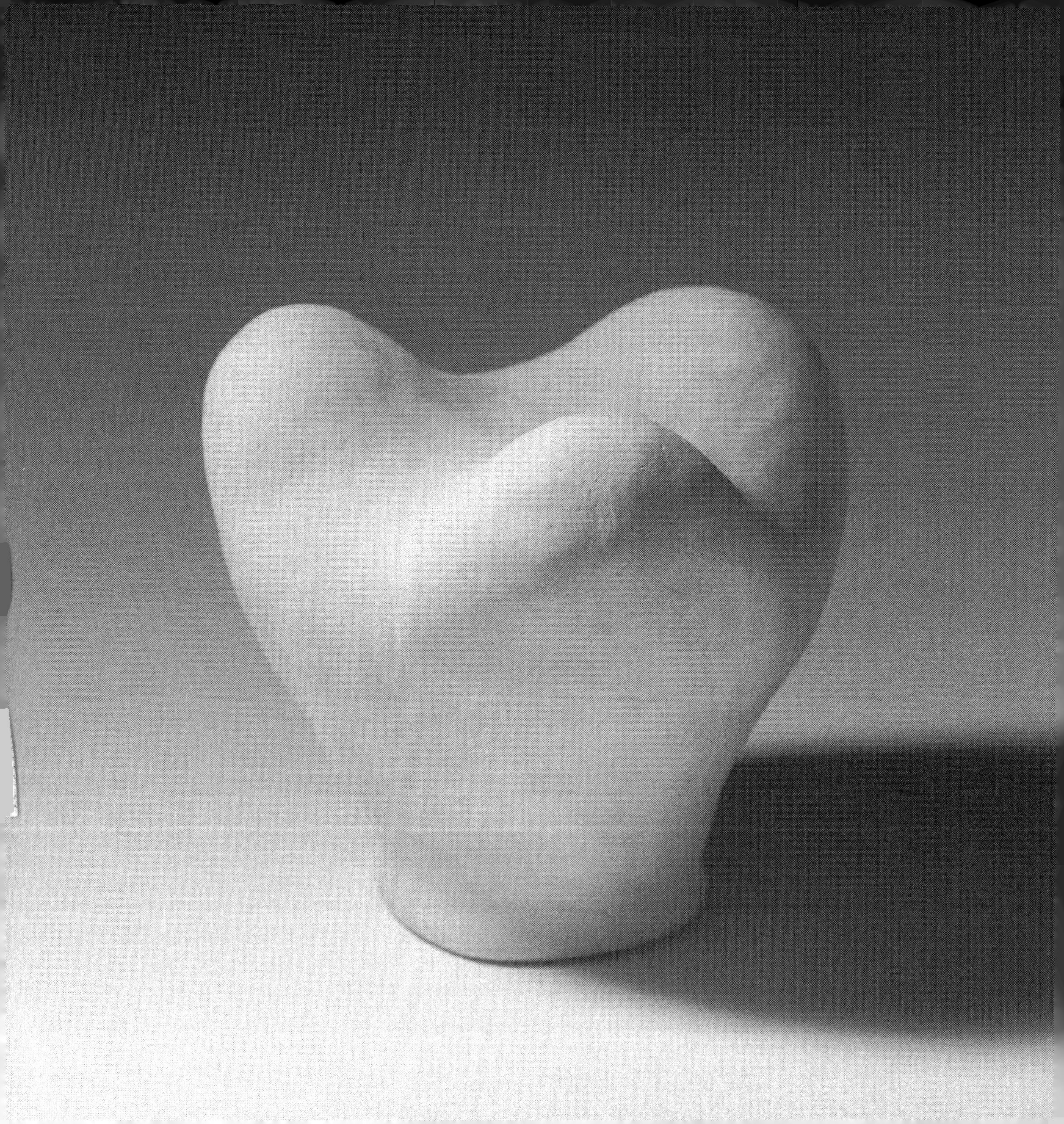

9. Threefold Symmetry Form: Stretching, Base and Foot

*The form so far appears somewhat coarse and still has a rounded base.
It is now slowly stretched around the vertical axis, then put down firmly,
grounded to give it a flat base. As we finally shape a foot, the sculpture
gains lightness resulting in a stronger relationship with the space around it.*

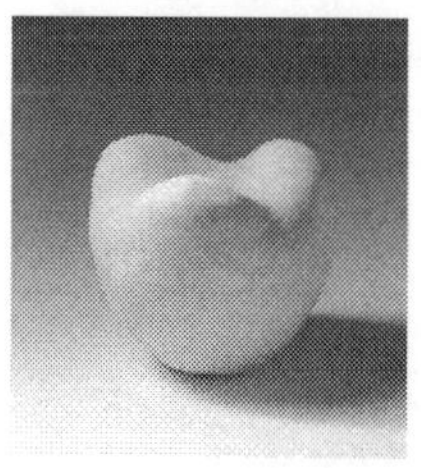

After I have practiced shaping the threefold symmetry form repeatedly with the children, until most of them can rather skillfully produce it, I proceed one step further. To better explain this next step, I want to call again attention to the fact that our work so far has taken place balanced at the approximate level of the heart. Off and on we have looked at the forms resting on our outstretched hands. Many of the forms have had fully rounded bottoms; some forms were slightly pushed down so they would stay upright. The next step involves further detaching from the form, with which the child so far has felt closely connected. The child will now learn to view his or her modeled forms from a greater distance as objects in space.

The teacher must watch for the right time for this step to a new awareness. Sometime during the third grade, the class will be ready for this step. Steiner has characterized this developmental phase as "crossing the Rubicon." In dealing with the third grade, I have consistently found Steiner's thoughts to be true: "Therefore it is of essential importance what kind of attention one directs to each single child and to the class as a whole. At this point in time the child quite inevitably approaches the teacher with questions. Neither the content of these questions nor the answer given to them matter as much as a certain awareness that gradually dawns upon the child's soul. This awareness springs from an indefinable element, which at this particular time has to develop between the teacher and the child. This is what the child feels: 'Up to now I have always looked up to my teacher. Now this is not possible without knowing that my teacher looks up to something that is higher than himself, to something that is rooted in the essence of life itself.' The child between the ninth and tenth year does need that, and it is connected with a growing inner turn towards objectivity. Until now the child actually has not distinguished between himself and the world out there, the environment. He now feels an increasing need to become an individual, which has boundaries, an inner-centered person facing the world out there."[14]

When I have concluded that my third grade has arrived at this turning point, I will observe the children enthusiastically practicing singing in rounds or songs in two voices. They are also ready to find new ways of sculptural modeling. I ask them on our practice day to take their threefold forms into their outstretched hands with the round bottoms pointing down, guiding them as follows: "You can now start to stretch your form downwards using the strong middle part of your hands [the metacarpal bones] just like we previously practiced with the three-dimensional oval. So you slowly turn your form around the imaginary vertical axis while pushing it like this, keep turning it and push again. That is how you stretch it little by little. The upper part does not change."

After the children have worked on this for a while and the forms have become more slender towards the bottoms, I encourage them: "Now set your form firmly and upright onto the table! Then kneel down and look at it closely from all sides." When placed on the surface firmly, their forms receive discernible flat bases. With more slenderness, the bottoms gain a certain lightness, which the children had previously experienced when modeling the right–left symmetrical shape out of an oval, but at that time rather unconsciously. This threefold symmetrical form has gained a new relationship to the space surrounding it, which the children experience with joy and satisfaction. This experience plays an important role during the review on the next day.

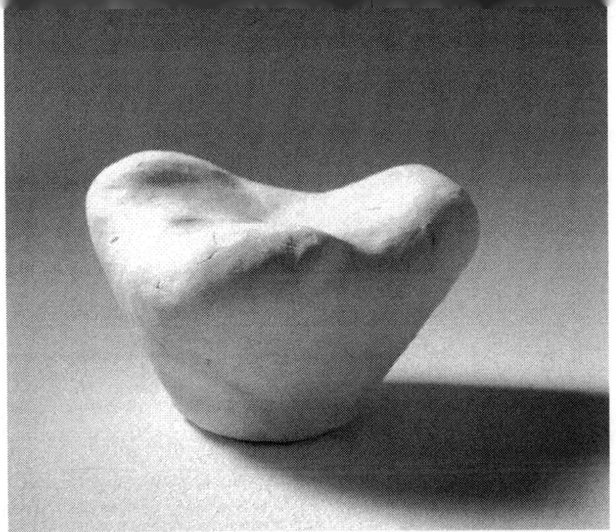

Rather willful but harmonious work by a girl

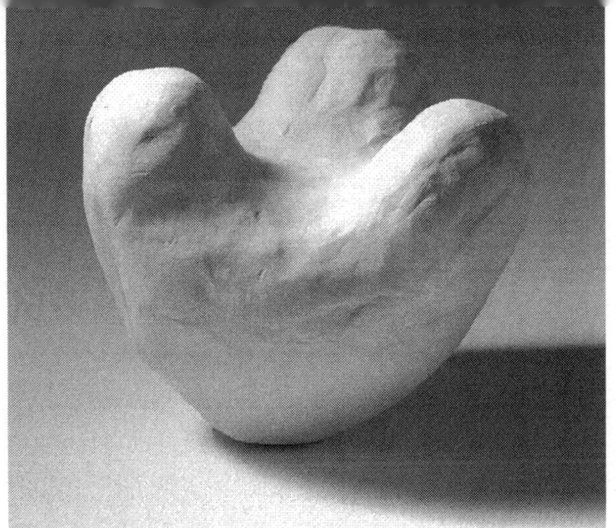

Vigorous form by a boy showing a strong will. The finer surface work was neglected in favor of the strongly expressive whole form.

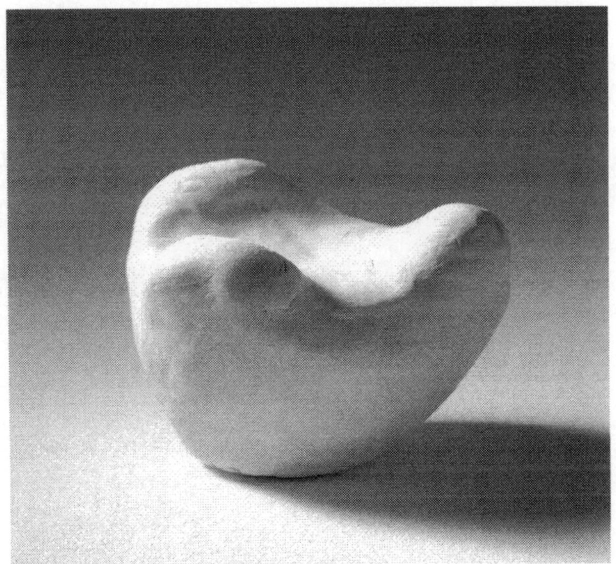

Visible stretching of the lower, previously rounded half of the form and a soft, opening gesture in the upper part; work by a boy

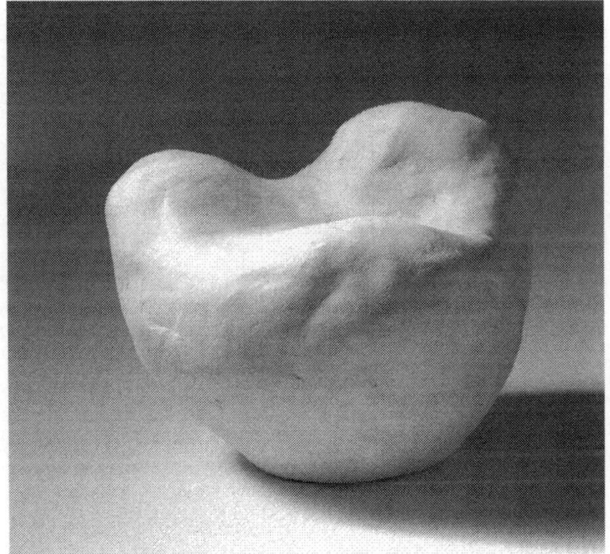

Vigorous, well-stretched work created by a boy. Repeated practice allows the children to produce increasingly harmonious forms of threefold symmetry.

For the next lesson I let the children shape another form of the threefold structure and ask them again to stretch it downwards, but more strongly than the first time. They take care to not let the form lose fullness in the upper part while stretching the bottom part more vigorously, which is not easy to do.

Like the last time, the form is then firmly set down and viewed from all sides. "How beautiful it would be if these forms had yet a little more lightness!" This comment was the result of our group review. "But how can we accomplish that?" some asked. In response I show the children how they can shape with their thumbs a foot, consisting of a band worked into the clay, just about one centimeter in breadth and inset by just a few millimeters at the bottom rim of the form.

The effect of such a technique is amazing: the form stands upright and firm on the surface, but it appears more graceful and lighter than before. It now is truly in relationship with the space surrounding it.

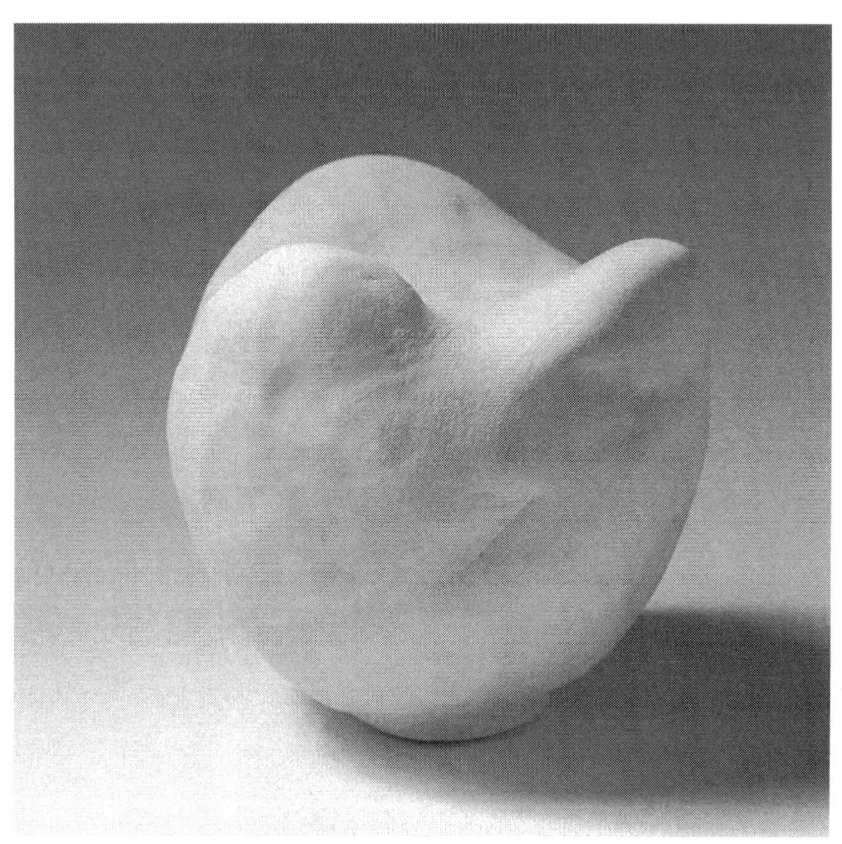

Here the threefold symmetry has been formed with sensitivity and gentleness, but so far the form has hardly been stretched. It still appears very spherical, but the foot is visible.
The work of a girl.

The children see this. The experience of this new spatial relationship can be deepened for the children by going back to such difficult formations as the flattened sphere or the sideways resting form with two saddle planes. As they repeatedly create such three-dimensional forms, the children are encouraged during the modeling exercises to check them out from a distance for shape, balance, lightness, and heaviness, and in so doing have many new important experiences with these forms.

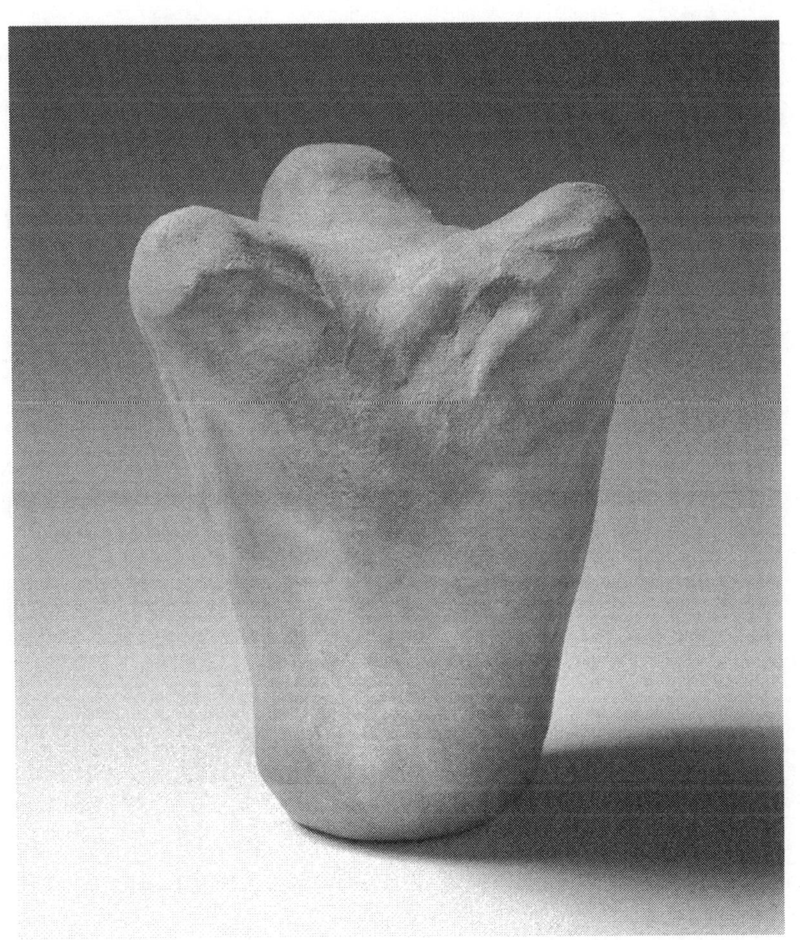

This boy has stretched his form more forcefully than others and has also given it a harmonious differentiation. This requires not only a good sense of form but also a strong will force and much patience. These characteristics were also evident in nearly all his other classes.

*Work of a nine-and-a-half-year-old girl. This model is
exceptionally beautiful, shaped with artistic sensitivity and a fine
sense of form. In reviewing the pieces the day after the modeling
session, many children can recognize the harmony and beauty
of such a sculpture. It motivates them to also try to create such a
beautiful form on the next practice day.*

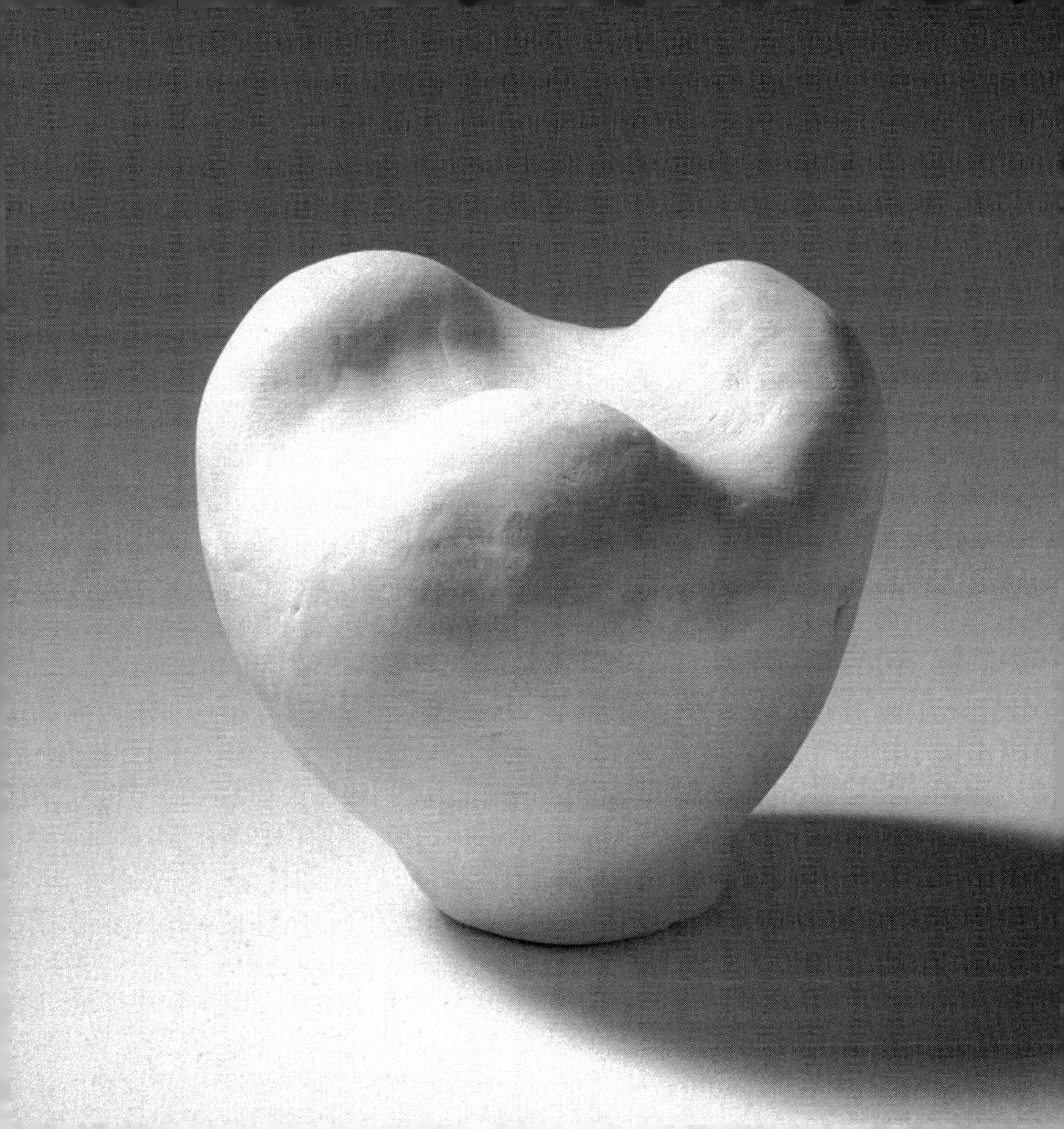

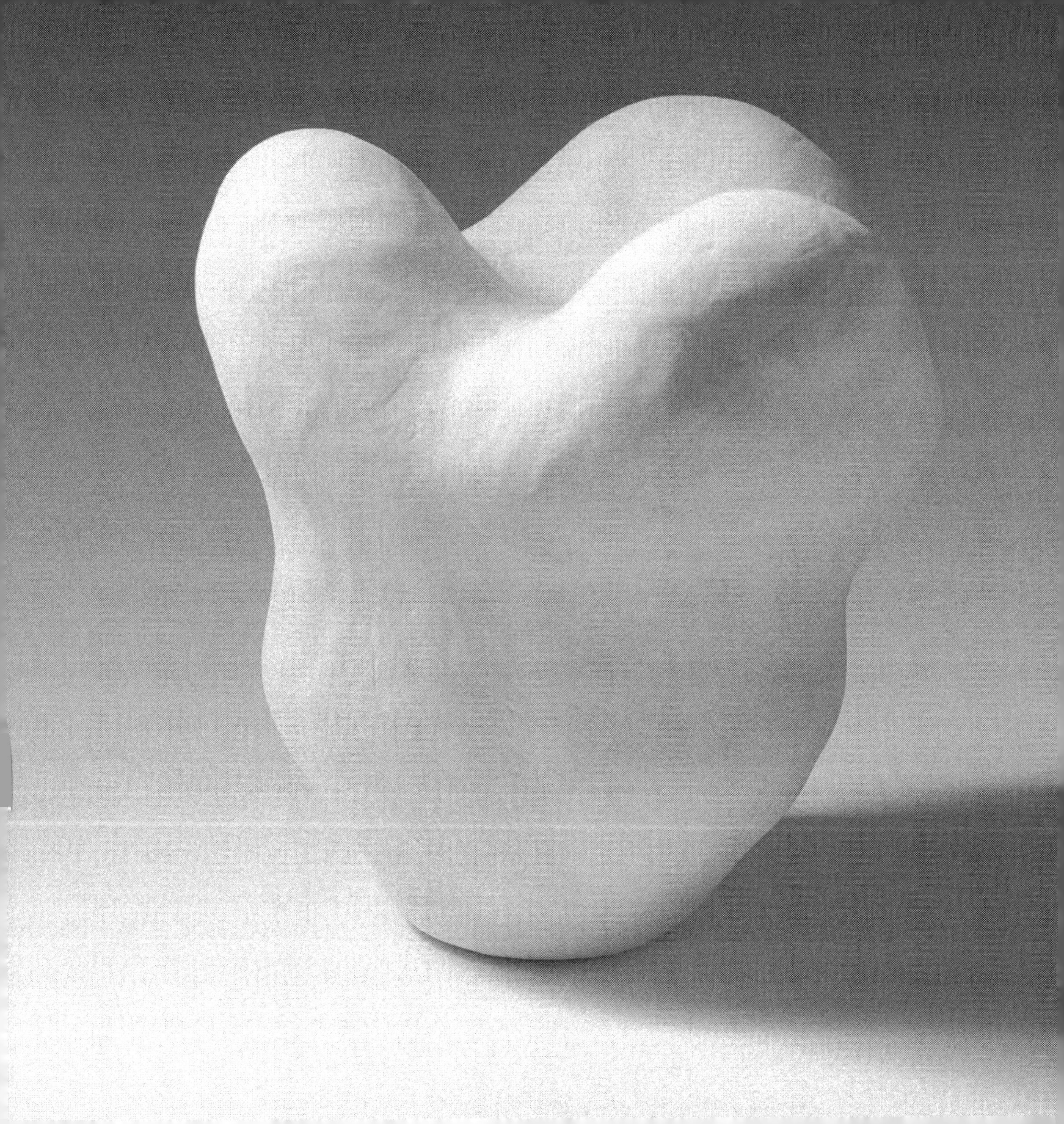

In subsequent exercises, I show the children how they can give an even more vivid structure to their familiar threefold symmetrical forms. This requires a further downward, vertical stretching of the form they have practiced so far (the direction of the applied pressure is horizontal), while retaining the fullness in the upper part of the form. I demonstrate how with the thumb and the ball of the thumb I can work another indent into the middle part of the form, below the threefold top, working all around the middle of the piece, and then again creating beautiful transitions. Moreover, creating smooth transitions between this indent and the lower part of the form stretching out vertically can be quite well accomplished by first gently evening out this area with both thumbs, positioned next to each other, while little by little turning the form on the vertical axis.

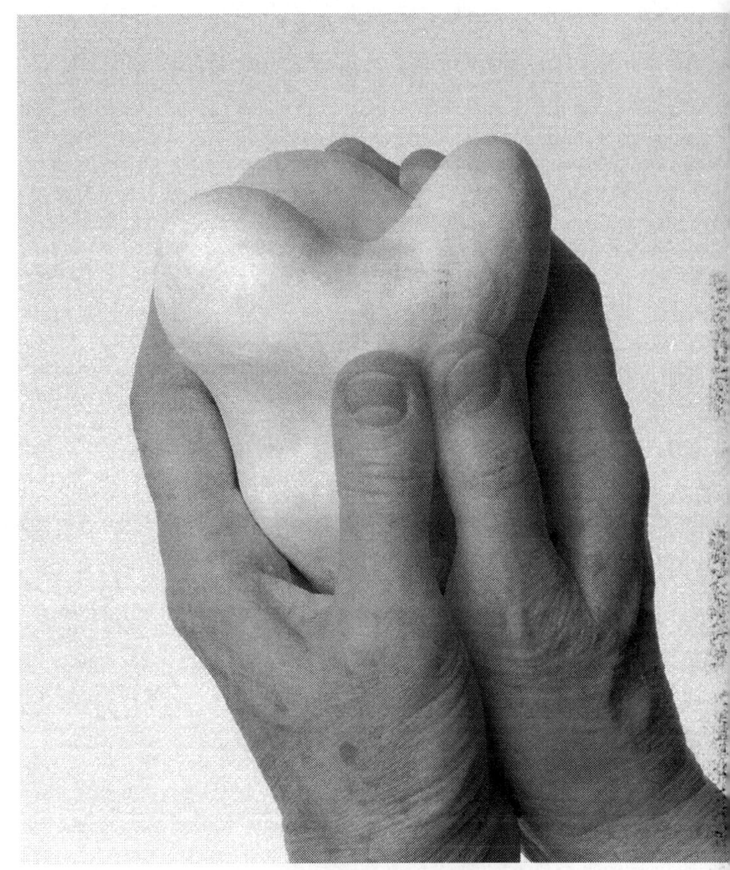

With the thumbs positioned next to each other we can work on further refining the hollow in the middle part of the form. For symmetry's sake, the form is continuously turned in this process bit by bit on the vertical axis.

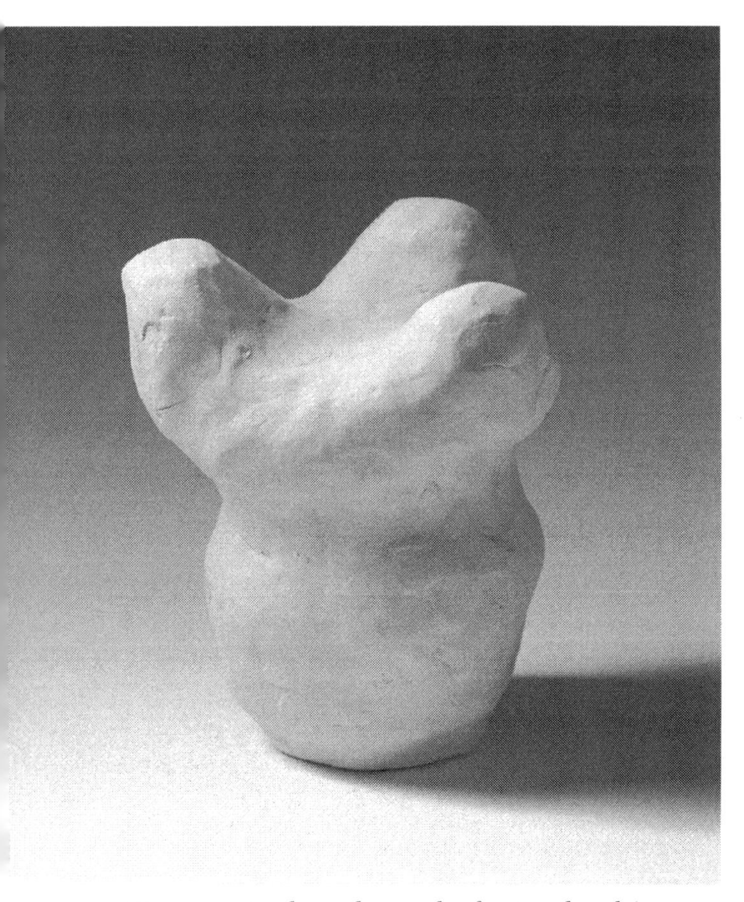

We recognize here the work of active hands!
Work of a nine-and-a-half-year-old boy

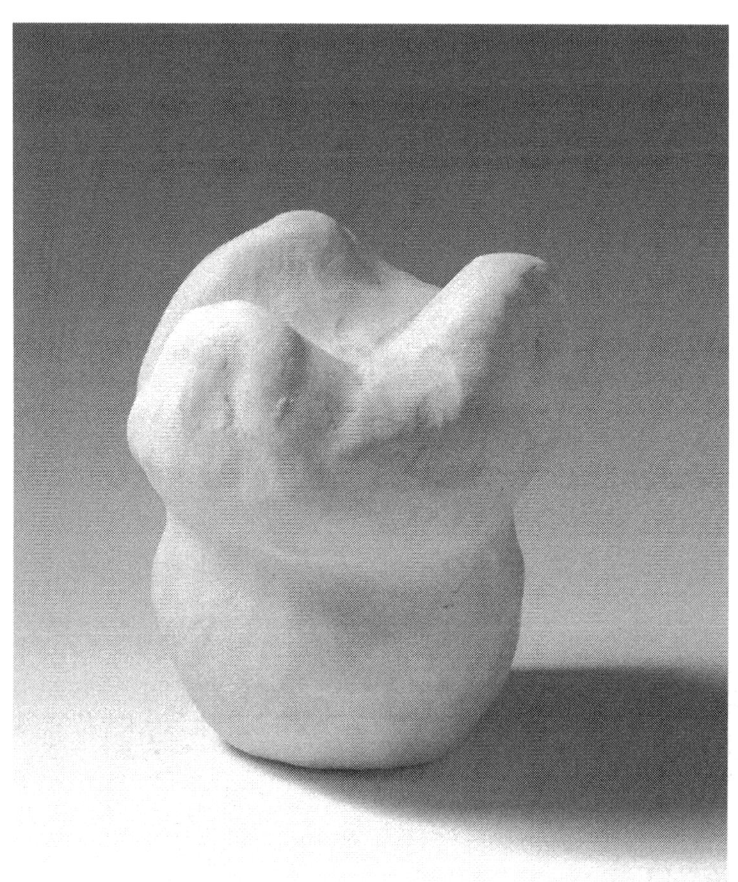

Work of a nine-and-a-half-year-old girl.
She has skillfully fashioned the form suggested
by the teacher. With repeated practice, she can
probably create even more beautiful transitions
between the double curved planes, rendering
the entire form more harmonious.

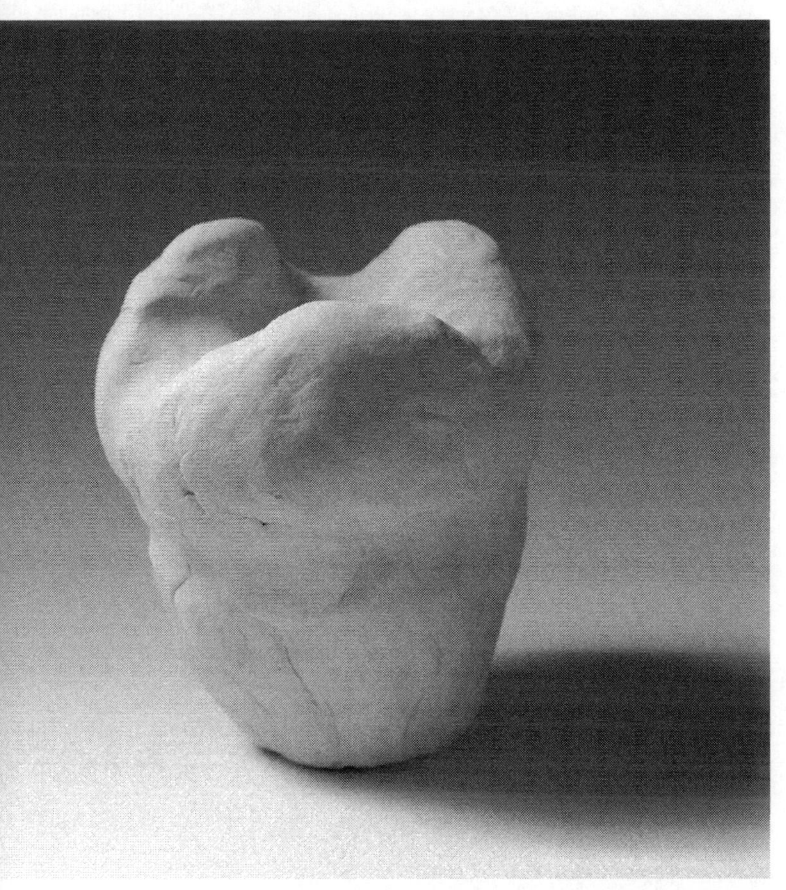

Work of a nine-and-a-half-year-old boy. Here we see a form with harmoniously created proportions. The next practice step for him will be to work the surface more delicately.

The details can be worked out afterwards with one thumb. Only a few particularly skillful children can succeed in doing all this the first time but, after a few practice sessions, many children acquire the knack for it. The pieces shown here demonstrate how diverse are the forms that the children create following the teacher's examples.

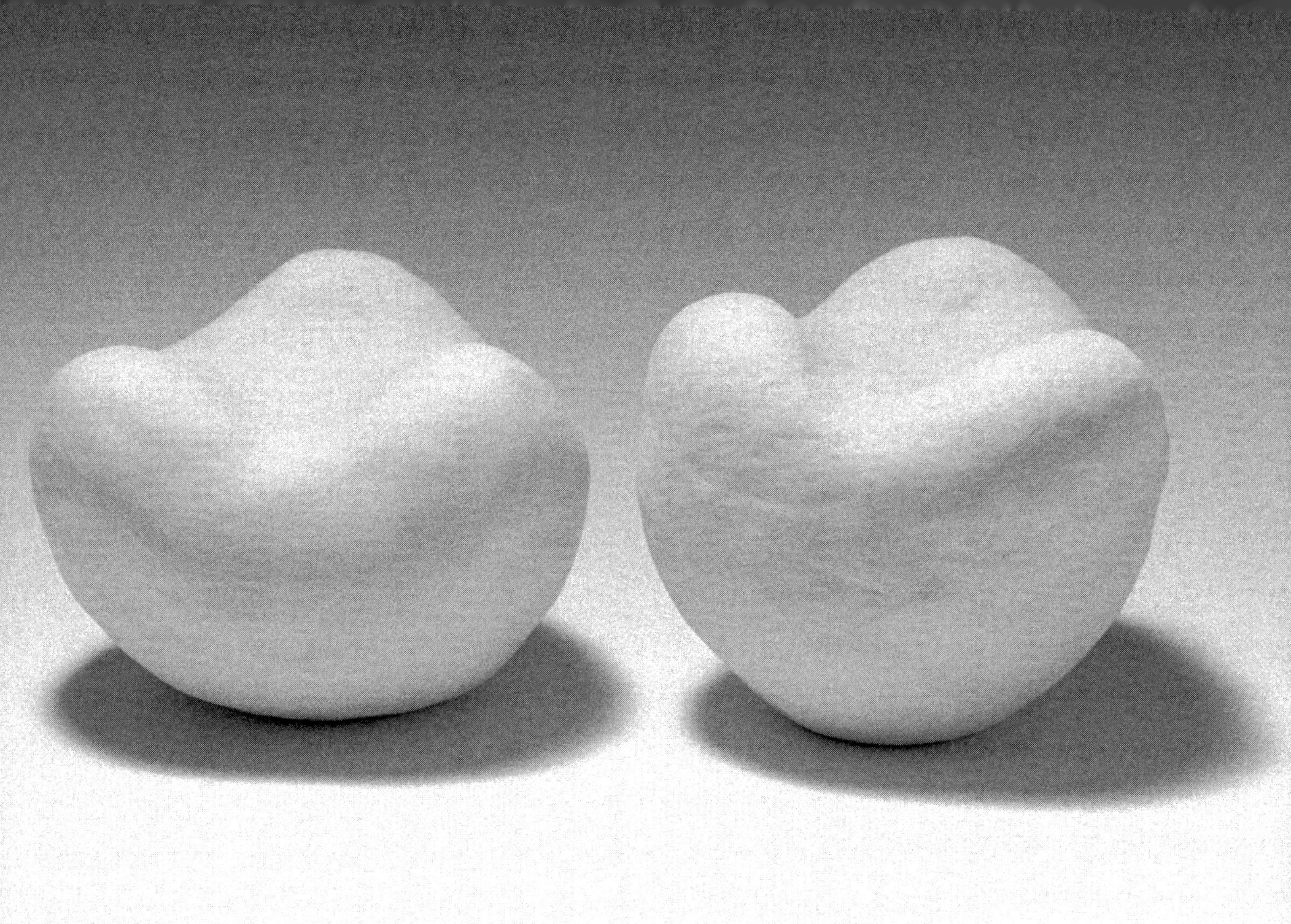

The series of threefold symmetrical forms are a lovely overview of the last part of the form series, which was developed together with the children. It illustrates how the shapes, all derived from the sphere, are created with increasing differentiation and how the modeling skills of the children develop.

70

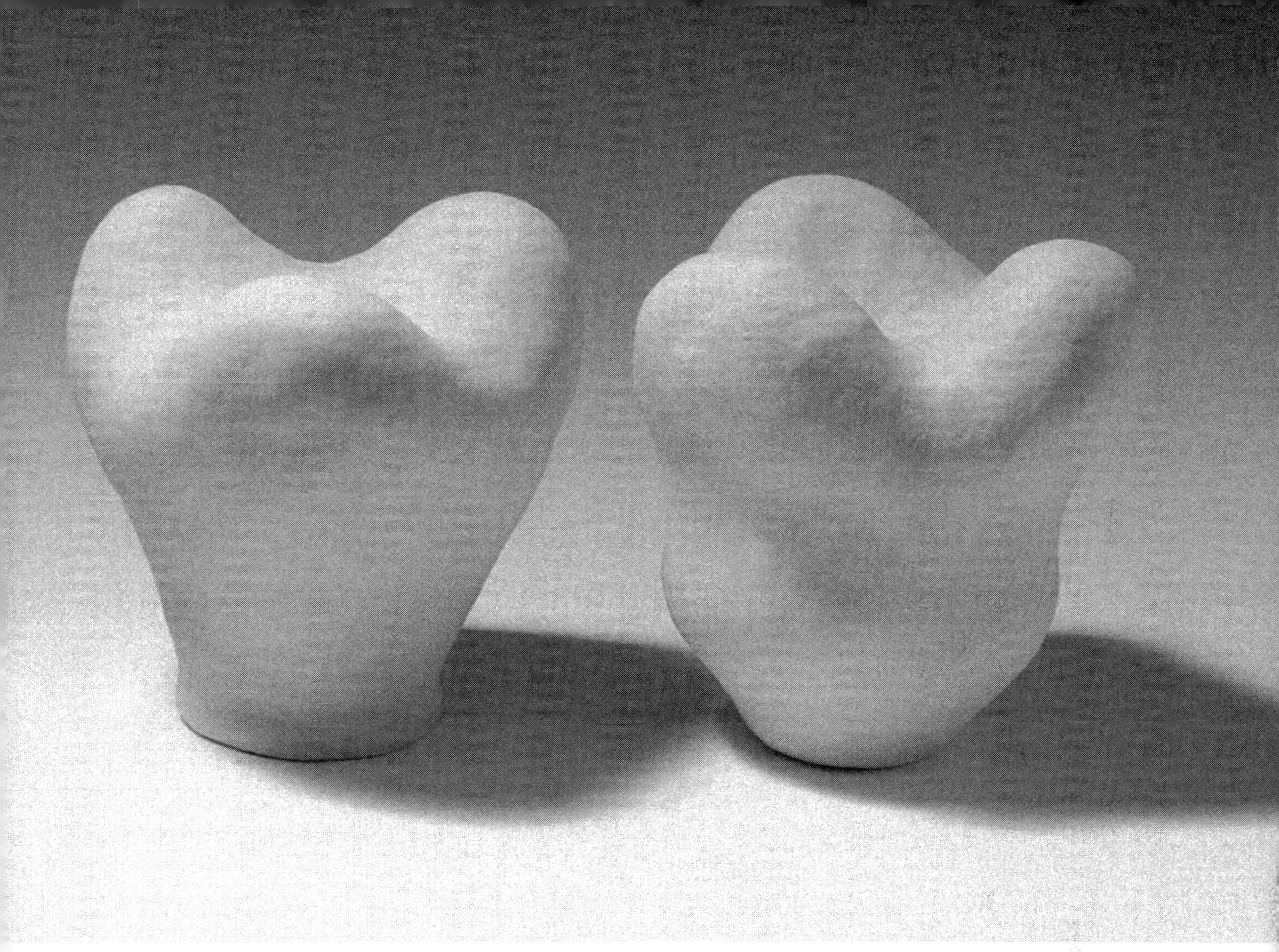

11. Looking Ahead to the Fourth Grade and Middle School (Grades 5–8)

The developmental stage of fourth grade age children is drastically different compared to previous years, and the curriculum of Waldorf education responds to that.

The children are now facing entirely new tasks in all classes – including the sculptural-pictorial arts. While their work in painting so far has been developed entirely out of the characteristics of the colors and remained mostly abstract, now they start painting animals and plants in their natural habitats. In their geography studies, natural scenes and moods at various times of the day or of the seasons make good topics for watercolor painting. The horizon, the transition between heaven and earth or ocean, always plays an important role too.

In connection with the Norse mythology, the students can experience a new artistic challenge in drawing various braided patterns. It is important to sharpen the awareness of a third dimension while dealing with lines; the spatial direction behind-in front is now added to the familiar spatial orientations of right-left and above-below. The forms of intertwined or braided bands or knots clearly help to develop this new faculty.

In modeling class from first grade on, the children have become familiar with three-dimensional forms. They have been able to acquire ever-finer sensitivities for sculptural forms and a growing awareness for three-dimensional space without copying shapes they find in the world that surrounds them. Now they can freely draw on this elemental sense for three-dimensional forms as they are guided towards new tasks in grades five through eight (middle school). There are many possibilities for such tasks.

Sculptural modeling can offer a wonderful enrichment for "the study of the human being" in the sense of the path which Steiner described in the lecture cycle *Kingdom of Childhood*.[15] Another field for applying modeling is the earth itself in environmental studies and geography. Valleys and hills of the children's immediate surroundings can be first characterized by the teacher in the fourth grade, then drawn as a simple map,[16] and finally explored with the children's own feet when hiking through the local area. Their whole being, especially their will-oriented life, is intensely and fully involved when they are afterwards allowed to model the valleys and hills in clay on their work boards.

A hands-on example from my own practice can help to illustrate this. During a sixth grade geography block I had described in detail to the students first the northern and southern limestone Alps and the crystalline central Alps, with each of their characteristic mountain formations and river valleys. Having drawn up a map of the Alps on the blackboard, and a few days later just a profile or cross section view of the Alps from north to south, I then asked the students to make a three-dimensional model of these Alpine formations in their distinct character. They were given plenty of clay and worked in pairs without any further instructions. The students worked with so much joy and creative enthusiasm that I was amazed. Their models were covered with damp cloths at the end of the main lesson period and were completed the next day. They tackled the task with an educated sensitivity for form and had by and large mastered it; it was apparent that hands had been at work that were experienced in sculptural modeling.

In Waldorf education, geometry is introduced to the students in the sixth grade. Until sixth grade the geometric shapes, circles, triangles, etc., are derived from drawing, after having practiced drawing in the early grades for learning to write. "Then we slowly progressed from the drawing we did for writing class to developing more complicated forms with the child. The painting and drawing classes in the fourth grade are directed into this sphere, and it is in drawing class that we come to teach what constitutes a circle, an ellipse, and so forth. We can advance this process further by always guiding the students towards three-dimensional forms, too."[17]

Now in sixth grade the students learn to construct geometric figures with compass and ruler, to describe the constructions verbally as precisely as possible, and to finally grasp them mentally. Modeling in clay again offers an ideal artistic means to grasp (in its original sense of the word) and to sense-feel three-dimensional forms. Starting again with the sphere, we can model in clay with the students first a cube, then the different pyramid shapes, the cone, the ellipsoid form and later, maybe in seventh grade, the more complex platonic solids.

In this connection it should be noted that Bothmer Gymnastics also uses geometric forms in working in the sixth grade, for example building triangles and quadrangles with staffs. [The Bothmer system is a framework of physical education generally practiced in Waldorf schools.]

III

PRACTICAL EXPERIENCES

This artistic practice of sculptural modeling based on Rudolf Steiner's suggestions is illustrated and described in this book using a concrete example from a first grade (Chapter I) and by introducing a sequence of forms (Chapter II). These chapters already provide various methodological hints for the teacher. In the following pages I will describe the essential pedagogical measures that I have tested hands-on in years of modeling with children.

1. The Preparation of the Teacher

The first step is the preparation for the class. For the work with the children to succeed, it is a basic requirement that the teacher familiarizes herself with shaping the elemental forms. This cannot be achieved by reading alone, but rather requires hands-on practice. If the occasion arises to take part in clay modeling classes offered by a sculptor, the teacher should take advantage of it; it would allow her to be acquainted with creative sculpting and to get stimulated artistically.

It is advisable to shape at least the sphere, alone and without any hurry, at the latest one day before the class and starting to work with clay for the first time in class – be it with a first, second or third grade. It is certainly of help to develop a clear awareness of one's own body posture and of all necessary movements and hand grips that one wants to use to instruct the children.

As I demonstrated in the two previous chapters, *how* the teacher speaks to the children plays an important role when she wants to inspire them to creative sculptural modeling. I do not use images of speech like I would do in a color story when watercolor painting with children in the first three grades. The point of modeling with clay is not to stimulate the children's fantasy, nor to instill in them any final images of the objects they are to form. The rationale for this work lies rather in inspiring the children to engage in very specific, subtle and differentiated movements, so that they can acquire a sense for elementary three-dimensional forms. Various methods can be used to achieve this goal.

The children of a first grade are engaged easiest in the intended motion sequence by the teacher's beginning to practice at the same time they do. Most children generally learn the new movements relatively quickly, thanks to their powers of imitation. I will accompany our common work together with a few verbal instructions. This methodical path was described through the concrete examples in Chapter I. The second way to familiarize the children with the new movements is to demonstrate them to the class while describing what I am doing. During this process the children sit quietly, relaxed in their places; maybe they just rest their lower arms on top of each other or cross them, so they can observe the teacher's movements with concentration. They do not yet touch their lumps of clay or their forms-in-progress. The quiet observance and listening process gives the children a first impression of the movements. When I ask them to make the same movements simultaneously with me, I set an impulse into the will of the child. This second method is appropriate for the second and third grades. But we also need to make some use of it when wanting to introduce a more complicated movement sequence or more difficult handgrips. How and when these two methodological approaches are applied depends of course on the frame of mind of the respective class we are teaching. Either way the motto applies: Demonstration is the method! The demonstration of the movements and the verbal instructions of the teacher are closely linked when we practice the three-dimensional form series, as in teaching any kind of handicraft. Therefore it is also so important to become aware of one's own way of speaking. The movement process while sculpting with clay can most vividly be described by using verbs such as "form, turn, rotate, press, stretch, push, even out, explore" and many others. The adjectives make the verbs subtler and differentiate them: "push gently, stretch carefully, turn slowly," and so forth.

The teacher should, if possible, avoid too many nouns, using them only when there is no better choice, for example "direction, bump, hollow hand, thumb." In order to educate ourselves in this way of speaking, we have to practice. That works best when the teacher retreats alone into a room, maybe into her classroom, and speaks out loud, underscoring her movements for shaping the form while holding in thought the children and directing her awareness to them so that she can show and describe the next hand movements, or let the children practice with closed eyes for a while, or maybe let them look at their work on the outstretched hand.

The teacher also has to think of what to bring verbally in the lessons, for example in language studies, and she has to prepare the storytelling material for the next day, not any easy task, but important for the success of a pleasant main lesson. The clay for the children should be portioned out and covered with damp cotton cloths either on the evening before the practice day or at least half an hour before the children come into the classroom; this is also part of the preparatory activities. The teacher also needs to provide buckets, towels, and cleaning rags for hand washing and cleaning the tables after the modeling class. When these various steps are considered ahead of time, the teacher will have the necessary assurance to meet the children serenely and confidently and will be able to react with aplomb to any unexpected happenings.

2. The Children Form Habits

So that instruction can take place at all a first grade class has to learn certain habits. They have learned already during the first practice days of watercolor painting, which generally precedes the modeling classes, that the sponges, water, brushes and colors may only be touched and used after the teacher gives the agreed-upon sign. If this behavior is already evident, the children in modeling class will have no difficulty touching the clay resting in front of them on the work board only when the teacher permits it.

The children should receive such instruction with benevolence and calm and, most importantly, the rules need to be implemented accordingly. If a child cannot keep to this agreement, there must be consequences. The children love clay modeling, and so it is a painful experience if they are not allowed to join the modeling activities during that day, because of their undisciplined fiddling with the clay before the class started. Such a child then gets a sheet of art paper and wax crayons and can draw while the others go through the modeling exercises. The children learn from such consequences with amazing speed!

Another habit the teacher instills in the class while modeling with clay is: "The mouth is silent while the hands do the work!" This is the most important of the golden rules mentioned earlier. The children comply with this rule readily – but for another reason. Although the teacher can not permit violation of this rule either, the true reason for a great, full silence spreading in the classroom shortly after the modeling class begins lies in the fact that the children experience a distinct sense of well-being during the quiet but intense work with the clay. They do not seem to have such a strong need for talking anymore. It is a different situation when the children place the unfinished forms on their outstretched hands during the exercise and look at them. Then a short conversation among the children is permitted and appropriate and also between the teacher and the children. The children quickly learn to differentiate these various situations and to respect the rules.

After the children have etched their initials with their thumbnails into the bottoms of their forms, reliable helpers can gather up the pieces. In the following minutes the teacher has to closely watch if the rules are obeyed that have been set for the cleanup phase; otherwise chaos is predictable! That means: The remaining clay stays on the art boards until gathered up by the helpers and taken to the clay container. The boards remain on the desks until the helpers collect them. While some wipe down the tables as fast as possible, the others can wash their hands in the buckets positioned on four chairs close to the blackboard. Soap is not necessary, and the towels are draped over the backs of the chairs. The better we have considered and organized the clean-up phase in advance, the less we will have to deal with nasty surprises.

By standing in front of the classroom with her back to the blackboard, the teacher can keep her eyes on the helpers and especially on those children who have nothing to do during these minutes. Otherwise she risks everything going topsy-turvy and clay on the floor, instead of in the clay container, and children just running wild. She must not under any circumstances let it get to that. The questions, "How do we deal with the materials after the exercise is finished," and "How do we maintain the necessary discipline?" are just as valid during modeling classes as during watercolor painting classes – it is really possible to get a grip on that.

3. Follow-Up for a Modeling Exercise

The follow-up for the modeling exercises can be extraordinarily insightful for the teacher. She comes to know a lot about each child as she contemplates unhurried and by herself the children's clay forms after the class. The work pieces reveal to the teacher how attentively each child has followed instructions, how skillfully or clumsily, patiently or impatiently he or she has formed the material and how sensitively or coarsely he or she has dealt with the clay. Often she can recognize how much emotion or aggression, which compels a child, has flowed into the form. Over time the teacher learns to read the individual modeling language of each child, just as one can learn much about their natures and also their temperaments through their watercolor paintings. For pedagogical reasons as well as for economy of time, teachers are well advised to review the clay forms right away on the day following the exercise together with the children, just like one generally does with watercolor paintings after each painting class day. The forms are already set out on the teacher's table, visible for all, when the children enter the classroom. The interested children can already take a look at all forms, without touching them.

After the rhythmical beginning section, i.e. after speech and music exercises, the teacher asks the children *how* the clay was modeled and formed during the previous day. She does not ask *what* has been formed. She has one child give a short verbal description of the process, perhaps several children. In a first grade class, she can help the children to find the appropriate words. When the process is recalled into awareness in this way, she can call up two or three children to come to the front table where the forms are set out. They are allowed to choose each two forms that attract their attention or that they like particularly and show them to the class by holding them up. If they express a wish to describe what they like about one or the other form and what attracted their attention, they are very welcome to do so. This exercise educates their language ability and form perception. The teacher will finally draw the attention to one or two forms and try to evoke in the children a joyous anticipation for the next modeling exercise. The difficulty during such a review is that not all children can look at all forms all at once, while they can see all the watercolor paintings hanging on the wall after painting class and might thereby be more easily drawn into the review process. This follow-up review should not take more than ten or fifteen minutes, rather less in a first grade class.

4. Time Management and the Principle of Repetition

Let us look at a possible schedule for modeling the form sequence over one school year, for example, in a first grade class. First is the choice of the day of the week. Monday is particularly well suited for modeling because we know that is the day of the week when the class is often difficult to teach in a way that is enjoyable for everyone. After the weekend the children return to school in widely varying, often quite unbalanced frames of mind, and the common modeling exercises can help harmonize the class community and prepare them to be receptive for further learning. Regarding the season: In Chapter VI there is a more detailed explanation, but basically fall and winter are particularly suited for the contemplative and quiet involvement with creative formative working in clay.[18]

The pedagogical principle of repetition plays an important role in regard to scheduling. Repetition is an indispensable condition for learning and finally mastering a manual skill. That is true for carving or knitting as much as for modeling with clay. By repetition I mean to remember movement sequences that were shown and performed one time, to retrieve them from memory and to revive them in a coordinated interplay of various sense functions. A first grade teacher should not hesitate to have the children repeat a form five times on consecutive practice days, for example when working with the three-dimensional oval or the first indent (saddle formation) into such an oval.

First the children should practice certainly more than five times shaping the clay into the basic form of all shapes, the sphere. The process of quietly exploring the clay through and through (as described in Chapter I) should always precede each exercise. The children need repetition to gain assurance and skill. Very few children in the first and second grades are able to model, after only a short practice period, beautiful, almost evenly formed spheres; the same is true for the three-dimensional oval shape. Those who are able to do that are rather quiet, reserved children who devotedly immerse themselves again and again in the formative process, even when it is only a repetition. The teacher should well consider before the class how she will vary and design – also in her verbal expressions – the exercises in such a way that they do not bore the children. But that is true for all teaching. If the teacher were to make twenty Mondays available for modeling, and if she chooses to use the form series introduced here as a basis for her work, she need not worry about being able to offer the children enough new impulses in modeling class. As we are practicing and learning the language of three-dimensional form, we discover many more possibilities to find abstract forms, starting from the sphere, along the lines of the examples shown here.

5. The Work Materials

Let me say now something in regard to the work materials used here. Plasticine, beeswax and mixtures of clay and beeswax – as they are prepared commercially – can be lovely, agreeable materials for sculptural modeling. One disadvantage is that often these materials are considerably more expensive than the fine, unfired clay for potters which is also excellently-suited for modeling exercises in the lower classes. The class teacher should compare prices and consult with art and craft teachers before purchasing material for the modeling classes. The clay is best kept in a large plastic box (isotherm container with a content capacity of about 50 liters) which has a vacuum lock, a box similar to those originally made for transporting perishable food items. This clay container is part of the permanent furnishings of my classroom.

The finished forms which are no longer needed will be broken up into small pieces while they are still damp and deposited in layers into the clay container, each layer being lightly sprayed with water, for example with a flower spray bottle. This treatment assures that the clay can have the right consistency on the next practice day. And that is definitely important! When the clay is too wet, it smears and clings to the hands and resists forming. If the clay is not damp enough, it dries quickly in the hands, and it is impossible to go on working with it. Usually the clay is of ideal consistency when we take it out of the sealed, plastic bag directly from the supplier, so one should strive to maintain that degree of dampness. During the first grade, the teacher will best break up the models herself, because the children cannot yet deal so well with the "destruction" of their pieces of work. Starting with the second grade a few children can assist in this process, probably outside of class time.

IV

How It Began

In summer 1986, for the second time, I took on a first grade class: 36 children in the Kräherwald Waldorf School in Stuttgart, Germany. Every first grade teacher knows that it is not easy for the children to integrate into the new large class community where they are faced with new challenges, even if they have experienced kindergarten. In this new class many diverse talents and the influence of various peoples, languages and religions were apparent. From this multicultural mixture arose visible, palpable tensions in the social interaction, which prompted several children to engage in violently aggressive behavior. Some children suffered serious physical injuries, others psychological anguish. The behavior of these children who were not yet ready for social integration made it difficult or impossible to teach meaningfully at the *beginning* of the main lesson period, that time span usually reserved for practicing common rhythmic movement, speaking and singing, mostly in a large circle. Also during the recesses in the schoolyard we often had to deal with extremely volatile situations. The usual pedagogical measures I tried did not suffice. I could not and would not tolerate this situation for very long. So the question came more and more urgently: How can the pent-up aggression expressed by these children (pushing, hitting, bullying and choking others) be redirected into a meaningful activity, especially since such behaviors most likely were not an expression of childish zest for action, but rather of fears and insecurities?

In response to this question I conceived of the following idea: I wanted to put into the hands of these children a compact, earthen substance that they could work on – it had to be earth, clay. Together with them, and not only them but with all children in the class, I wanted to model in clay.

Why modeling in particular? I was later asked. I knew what a pleasant, freeing effect sculptural modeling with clay can have, due to the fact that I myself had frequently and joyfully modeled with this material. I imagined how healing it could be, if the children with unacceptable behaviors could divert their pent-up aggression and fear and let them flow into the malleable material, into the clay that is pleasant to touch. I also counted on this activity to have a positive effect on the children if they were allowed to work with both hands. Being allowed to grip and work with both hands could help sensitize the inner parts of their hands. I hoped that such a guided activity of the will would be able to help the entire class. I thought the exercises would have to be artistic-therapeutic in content, if they were to be effective.

After I made this decision, I started to feel a strong sense of responsibility for the curriculum and to my colleagues. Why? To work with clay in the first grade was at that time – as far as I knew – not customary in Waldorf schools. Some class teachers let the students of the first and second grades form small figurines from beeswax in the pre-Christmas weeks. But only a few teachers regarded the modeling of elementary, abstract forms in clay in the first three to four grades as part of the art curriculum, and it was rarely done.[19]

Considering this background I am very grateful to the former faculty of the Kräherwald Waldorf School, who gave me express permission to take this unusual path with the children of the first three grades. My colleagues motivated my work and constructively questioned it, especially in the beginning phase, with very critical well meaning interest.

I shared my plans with an experienced professor at the Waldorf Teacher Training College in Stuttgart; she too had taught students of all age levels before starting to work at the College. At her initiative, a small group of colleagues started meeting shortly after I had started to do clay modeling with the children, and they participated in a pedagogical research project in the field of clay modeling in the first three grades. Among them were two more professors from the College who were also working in sculptural-pictorial arts. They encouraged me to do what I thought to be right and what circumstances required for these children even if it was not customary.

This working group, in which also three class teachers of other Waldorf schools joined, met only a few times in the course of three years. Nevertheless, we succeeded to pave the way for a methodical approach to modeling elementary forms with children in the lower grades – an approach that seeks to implement Steiner's indications. At each new group meeting, the practical pedagogical experiences which I had gone through with the children were taken into consideration. Simple, clear forms were developed that could be well-nestled in the hands of young children. Taking the age level of the children into account, we avoided all sharp edges, pointed and deeply hollowed out formations and inner spatial forms. Full, clearly organized forms were the result. Relief-type works and stacked forms on firm foundations were excluded from the path we wanted to take.

We continued to search for statements by Steiner in regard to sculptural modeling with clay for this age group, which eventually yielded important clues. Thus the foundation was laid for the form series, a selection of forms from the developmental process described above, complemented by a few forms that I have developed independently over the years, quite in keeping with previous cooperative work. This form series may be of service to interested teachers, possibly also to therapists and parents as inspiration for their own work with children.

About the class which prompted this pedagogical research work, I may report the following: The work in the field of sculptural-pictorial arts increased during the fall and winter months by adding regular modeling with clay and, as much as possible, we continued with the weekly painting class. The children continued form drawing in three- to four-week block lessons. This had a distinct harmonizing effect on the entire community of the class. The particularly aggressive children became increasingly more involved in the guided modeling activities and learned more and more to bridle their own wills.

V

About the Effects of Modeling with Clay

Over the course of many years of sculptural practice with the children, I have been able to observe the effects this artistic activity has on a class as a whole and also on individual children. I have perceived certain effects directly *during* the modeling process and *after* finishing the practice sessions. The latter is also true for the further course of the main lesson period and for some track classes that followed the sculpting sessions. Moreover, I assume that this artistic activity has an effect on the overall development of the children in the following weeks and months, although one cannot determine it with certainty, of course, since the modeling classes have to be seen in connection with the other subjects, which had an effect as well.

In this chapter I will describe first my own observations and towards the end also the perceptions of two colleagues from the Kräherwald Waldorf School. Let me emphasize that this book is not the result of a scientifically designed long-term study! It would indeed be desirable if the experiences we have gained so far would inspire as many teachers and therapists as possible to work with children in the way described here and to make observations in this process, to examine them and to write them down. That could lead to a further development and pedagogical recognition of this artistic activity with children in the first three grades.

I will briefly name and then later describe in more detail the various areas in which I have observed the impact of modeling exercises on the children. First, I want to point to the extraordinary harmonizing effect on a class community of thirty to forty children. The peacemaking effect plays an important role for the children who are particularly aggressive. In this regard one needs to pay attention to the fact that the exercises bring about a clearly discernible establishment of the breathing rhythm and, consequently, a thorough warming-up process pervades the entire group of children and each single child. Even though within this methodological approach, the children work in a sitting position and execute only relatively small movements with their arms and hands in contrast to the more generous rhythmical movements in the morning circle, these small movements nevertheless make the children breathe freely and easily.

Another observable phenomenon is the great joy which the children experience in connection with this artistic activity through the particularly intense tactile sensation in both hands. Modeling in clay quite probably also stimulates and benefits the metabolic processes, as it obviously quickens the entire sensory system, in particular the lower senses, the senses of will. Sculptural modeling is a predominantly inner-directed activity, proceeding quietly and contemplatively, while both hands learn finely differentiated movements. The tactile sense of the hands also undergoes a particular sensitization as well. This activity apparently generates a special openness for dealing in a qualitatively sophisticated way with the word and with language. Practical classroom experience has shown again and again that the children immerse themselves very sensitively and vividly in exercises involving both their mother tongue and foreign languages. It is difficult to assess what the impact is on later years in subjects like geometry or botany or high school artwork as a result of this development of the form-sense and of spatial awareness, which the children attain during the first school years. We still have too few experiences to ascertain such long term effects.

1. Harmonizing the Classroom Community and Making Individual Children More Peaceful

Fortunately, a first grade teacher experiences many occasions when the children are able to become engaged in tasks joyfully and eagerly. That is true for pictorial-artistic classes like watercolor painting or form drawing, and also for imaginative, rhythmic movement or circle games, accompanied by the children's speaking or singing. First and second graders listen with strong inner involvement to a fairy tale, a legend or a meaningful story, which the teacher tells freely and vividly, perhaps at the end of a main lesson. The class is a harmonious community in these times, be it in artistic activity or in a process of inner involvement, listening, absorbing.

The harmony pervading a class during a sculptural modeling class is qualitatively different from that in these class situations. The intense creative activity of both hands proceeds in healing and contemplative silence. First, the rhythmical, relatively strong movements of the hands, pressing and forming, visibly stimulate the circulation and at the same time challenge the will into creative activity. The subtler movements of thumbs and fingers require a very concentrated, sensitive type of work, for example, in attending to the beautiful design of the double curved planes or for evening out the model's surface. In the intense tactile sensing process the children derive a visible satisfaction because they experience themselves as individuals. Their self-assurance increases, and they experience a perceptible sense of well-being throughout their entire bodies. It is the sense of life, communicating to the person something about one's own inner bodily state. Steiner characterized this sense of life as the sense that is foremost for the sculptor that he uses and refines in order to create and perceive sculptures.[20]

One first grade boy in my class was having tremendous difficulties integrating into the community of the class. He was a mid-size boy, harmoniously formed and fine-featured, who showed alarming chaotic expressions of will, in particular at the beginning of the school day. He would grip another child by the throat and choke him vigorously. He might strike out blindly, sometimes with a full backpack. He would kick another child, another time knocking a tooth out of another child's mouth, and the next day pushing a classmate down the stairs. This boy was incredibly tense inwardly, he felt unsafe, fearful in regard to his entire social environment, and not only in school, which was probably the reason why he acted so aggressively towards his classmates. This boy willingly immersed himself in sculptural modeling exercises, but at first he worked the clay in such a way that he literally choked it with both hands. Within a few minutes, this made the clay dry out and crack so that it could no longer be formed. Each time this happened I quietly and calmly gave him a new portion of clay. Over the course of several weeks, this boy learned to let go of the tension in his hands during the modeling exercises to such a degree that he could work in a relaxed, even joyful, engaged manner. He became markedly more peaceful, outwardly and quieter inwardly. The groping, forming gestures in his work with the clay had given him the opportunity to store his fears and aggression into the material and to finally overcome them.

Another first grade student, a strong, somewhat stocky chap with red cheeks and flashing eyes, felt so frisky that he was not shy of starting fights during the break, even with students of higher classes, not to mention with his classmates. He had particular difficulties getting the hang of the common rhythmic movement, speaking and singing exercises in morning circle, and all too often he dampened the enjoyment of the other children in this work. But whenever we would practice sculptural modeling, this boy was always the most eager. He helped to distribute the art boards and the clay, and he eagerly helped with clean up. When engaging in clay modeling he could finally vigorously grip something with both hands and really get to work on it. He did not have an easy time molding his forms, and he had even more difficulties with finely evening out the surfaces – but he found visible satisfaction in this activity. His belligerence and insults declined markedly over the course of the school year. I gained the impression that the beloved activity of modeling in clay slowly and indirectly also opened the door for him to a fuller participation in the rhythmical exercises in morning circle.

2. The Warming Process

About four weeks after this first grade had started modeling in clay once a week, a child asked one morning, "Do you know that today we completely forgot our clay work?" Of course I had not forgotten the "clay work," as the children liked to call the modeling exercises. It had to be rescheduled due to an all-school festival. The child, who obviously valued modeling very much, was frail, light-blond, relatively tall for her seven-and-a-half years, slender and delicately formed and was of a shy and quiet disposition. I often observed in her signs of insufficient blood circulation; she looked pale, and her hands felt chilly at the morning

handshake and often even at the goodbye handshake. But this girl was very receptive and eager to learn. She participated joyfully in the music and speech exercises in morning circle, and, right from the beginning, she formed the clay with heartfelt devotion. It came to my particular attention that the carefully designed, beautiful forms of this child were quite warm in comparison to others, and the clay was not dry at the end of the practice period. During the modeling exercise her cheeks would turn red and her hands warmed up. Apparently the breathing and the warming processes in this child were stimulated in a particularly effective way, which probably contributed to her love of modeling activity.

We can experience in our own bodies (and it has been scientifically proven) that movement leads to increased blood circulation and that will activities result in warming processes. Modeling in clay, this relatively quiet activity of the will performed with both hands, can be viewed as a special case within this general law, for it is a practice in which a differentiated and individual warming process takes place. All children receive a piece of clay of the same room temperature, and all of them work in the same external environmental temperature, i.e., within the classroom. At the end of the activity all forms are warmer than the originally distributed clay, but they show distinct differences in warmth and dryness. I have concluded that in no case do the children in the lower grades suffer because of the damp, initially cool clay. The concern that the children's bodies could lose warmth when modeling in clay has no basis. Rather, the children work joyfully and with true enthusiasm, if they are guided accordingly. Secondly the clay warms up quickly during the work process. They all have warm hands and most have red cheeks, even for up to an hour after the modeling exercises. All the handshakes at the end of the modeling class are warm!

As adults we can become aware of the phenomenon of self-warming when working with clay in a circle. After each participant finishes a form, he or she passes it on to the neighbor, who can now feel the warmth as well as the artistic design of the form. This can be continued until all participants have held each form in their hands. This is an amazing experience! The forms feel distinctly different, from lukewarm to extremely warm with many gradations of warmth in between, but all sculptures are distinctly warmer than the clay at the beginning of the exercise. This exercise with young children in a large class could create too much excitement and disquiet. With children, the test of warmth is more meaningful when limited to comparing the temperature of the initially portioned-off piece of clay with that of the finished form.

3. Touch Experience: The Development of the Sense of Touch

As the intense touch-experience pervades the entire process of sculptural modeling, it is not easy to look at separately. But compared to other manual skills or formative-pictorial exercises, we can clearly see the difference between these in regard to the sense of touch.

Children in the Waldorf first grade learn to knit, and nearly all children take a particular liking to this activity. They use both hands for that activity. Knitting requires "extremely complicated fine-motor movement sequences of the right hand in exact coordination with the left hand"[21] when forming a loop from a finely spun, continuous thread and adding this loop to the other knitting stitches. Repeating this process many times over, they create a continuous, flat piece of knitting. In particular, they use the fingers of both hands, engaging them in practical, intelligent activity, both index fingers taking the lead and the thumbs and other fingers holding the knitting piece in place. In this process the children have only a partial touch experience, where the fingertips touch the needles and the yarn or the whole piece; the inner parts of the hands are barely involved.

In painting and drawing, the thumb, index finger and middle fingers of one hand guide the paintbrush or pencil, which results in a touch experience only at the point where the tool is touched. The picture or drawing emerges outside of the hands on a plane, on the paper, positioned in front of the child. The children touch the paper only indirectly, just by the pen or brush.

Neither in knitting nor in drawing or painting does the child experience such an immediate and complete tactile sensation as during modeling with clay. First, we have only an unformed, compact mass of clay. What follows is first a subtle tactile exploration of the clay, bit by bit, with the thumb, the index and the middle finger, a first process. After that, the clay is gripped all around with both hands and formed. Both hands in threefold organization have to become active in this process. The fingertips [the nerve-sense pole] are needed for the subtle tactile exploration of the clay and for refining the form's surface design. The metacarpal bones and the palms [the sphere of sense experience] are needed for tactile pushing, stretching, surrounding and for the "blind" tactile exploration of a form; these parts of the hand become tremendously agile and alive in this process. We use the ball of the hand or the thumb [the willing pole] for vigorously imprinting, indenting, shaping saddle planes, for particularly forceful pushing and forming steps. Throughout the entire work process both hands are in direct contact with the piece, in various positions and movements while feeling, touching, forming but without engaging in a continuous repetitive series of movements. The form emerges as a three-dimensional figure within the hands. On one hand we experience the outer world through these differentiated tactile processes (warm or cold, damp or dry, pliable or resisting), and we experience the entire emerging form. On the other hand we become aware of the inner world of ourselves through contemplative inner activity, which can bring deep satisfaction and joy, inner harmony, and bodily well-being. Children have this experience just like adults.

4. The Stimulation of the Metabolic Processes

One first grader who had always been sickly told his mother and me with deep conviction, "Form modeling is much more beautiful than even painting!" This boy had a congenital metabolic insufficiency, in particular a weakness of the liver function. He also suffered from rachitis. Although he learned to walk at the right time, he was slow to speak and had difficulties talking. Between the ages of two-

and-a-half and four, he underwent a chirophonetic treatment to support his language development. In the second seven-year period of his life, this boy continued to struggle with his weak constitution. Consequently he had been in continuous pediatric care and depended on regular medication and special nutrition. He always tired quickly, but had trouble falling asleep at night.

He entered the Waldorf school at the age of six-and-three-quarter years, but in contrast to most of the children in the class he showed no real enjoyment of learning. Yet he expressed much affection for the teacher and often greeted her twice in the morning with a cordial, firm handshake. School probably altogether was too much of an exertion for him. He made a strong initial impression on me. His rhythmic movement, speaking, and singing in morning circle were awkward. All tasks challenging his faculties of imagination and thinking were extremely difficult. There were only three subjects he really enjoyed in the first years of school and in which he enthusiastically participated: the movement game class (erroneously called play gymnastics), painting, and modeling with clay. Up into the fourth grade, this boy had the opportunity to regularly engage in modeling with his class once a week in the winter months. Toward the end of the fourth grade he slowly learned to write and read the words with all the required syllables, but he was not yet able to grasp grammatical forms and rules. He did comprehend calculating with abstract numbers and the introduction of fractional arithmetic. In the following years this boy made good progress in his physical body and in soul and spirit; he was able to complete his high school education and graduate after twelve years. In summary we can say that this child could not take hold of his cognitive faculties for a long time, a difficulty certainly related to the grave weakness in his metabolic-limbic system. While this child instinctively avoided all types of exertion, he approached those tasks which provided him with an experience of physical well-being, strengthening his metabolic processes. Based on this one report we cannot draw the conclusion that modeling has a therapeutic effect on a medically diagnosed metabolic weakness. But I nevertheless described this case here in order to inspire and challenge teachers and therapists to explore this possibility with more detailed observations in this regard. Is it possible that the activity of the inner organs, for example the intestinal peristaltic, is beneficially stimulated through clay modeling experiences? Is it possible that development and improvement in the metabolic-limb system might be brought about by the rhythmically impulsed pushing, groping and forming movements of the modeling process?

5. The Stimulation of Language Abilities

It is generally accepted that the movements of the hands and fingers have significance with regard to the stimulation of the language sphere. Does sculptural modeling have a very specific effect in this connection? To answer that question we would need to examine the subtle stimulation and sensitization of the inner hand and the tactile sense in general, which is very much trained in the modeling exercises described in this book. We then would need to ask what impact the development of these skills might have in regard to supporting our language faculties, our ability to listen and to speak out loud. This connection has long been a subject of scientific research. "But if the faculties of movement are not properly developed, then we will probably also find deficits in the sensory faculties. That was in particular proven for the sense of touch: children age three to six with a healthy development of language showed in Kiese-Himmel's tests significantly higher scores in tactile- and touch-awareness than other children of the same age group who demonstrated speech particularities. The latter were still overtaxed during follow-up tests in the second grade, when faced with complex tasks involving tactile awareness.

Accordingly, the full development of our tactile sense seems to be a necessary preliminary condition for language acquisition in the child."[22] Again and again I have observed how children can listen more thoroughly and sensitively to the language-oriented tasks during the classes immediately following the quiet modeling exercises.

There is a real appetite in first graders, for example, to truly taste certain sounds, harmonies and melodies of speech in words and rhymes. Here is a small sketch: "Fleeting fish flit through the flowing flood waters … fleeting, finch, fish, wish … flitting, flying, fluttering … bubbles, bells and balls – trucks, tracks and trolls – lice and fleas, mice and bees, pepper and peas… ." There are so many possibilities to gather words, word sequences and rhymes on certain sounds! How the fountainhead of speech starts to flow! Here we can experience in the children the transformation of the previous form-giving movement into a creative sound movement.

Another example – this one taken from a third grade – further illustrates this observation: A frail, extraordinarily shy girl, an only child, and who had never attended kindergarten did not ever during the first two school years dare to answer any question or even contribute one single sentence to the retelling of a fairy tale or a story. The only exception was her standing directly close to me in second grade and dutifully reciting in a low voice her report verse.[23] This child was however by no means intellectually slow or mentally sluggish. She participated regularly in the common exercises of speaking and singing. All written assignments indicated that she followed the lessons very attentively and with understanding. In form drawing she produced a delicate sense of form and surprised me by her clear, assured line drawing. In third grade, shortly after the Christmas vacation, the very first grammar language block ever was supposed to take place. It was a Monday morning, and as usual in the winter months, the class had first gone through exercises in modeling with clay. Immediately after these exercises, the teacher asked that they engage in saying out loud meaningful question and exclamation sentences. The teacher reminded the children of the fairy tales they had heard in the first grade. She posed questions like: "In the fairytale of Snow White, how did the dwarfs talk after they returned home and noticed that someone had touched their things?" And, "What did Little Red Riding Hood say when she saw her grandmother lying sick in her bed, having such strangely big eyes, ears and hands?" This child, who had never before even wanted to speak alone in class, was the first one to raise her hand this morning, and she answered with a complete sentence, clearly and succinctly. This miracle happened one more time, just a few minutes later! From that day on the girl was no longer shy, she said what she knew, courageously and clearly. Now one could deny that this child would have taken this important developmental step anyway between her ninth and tenth years, even without the sculpting exercises. But it is remarkable that she had obviously been motivated to courageously answer the questions by the preceding activity and stimulation of both hands. It is obvious that the form-giving modeling gesture was transformed into a soul-infused experiential gesture of language.

6. Observations from Colleagues

The colleague who taught a foreign language to these children starting in first grade, is richly experienced in foreign language instruction on all class levels. He implemented a comprehensive research study in the area of teaching foreign languages in the early grades so I felt I could rely on his perceptions and reports. This colleague was rather astonished when he experienced my class on a Monday morning right after they had done sculptural modeling for the first time during main lesson period. He reported to me that he had found a much improved work atmosphere. On many subsequent Mondays, he also observed that the children were much more focused after having done modeling exercises, that they were more at peace in themselves and were much more incarnated in their bodies than on other days.

Some weeks after introducing sculptural modeling with clay in the first grade, the school physician came to visit during a Monday morning main lesson. She had many years of experience observing children of this age group. She had also come to know these particular children before they entered the school and knew about the concerns I had in regard to several of them. So she was with us on that Monday morning when the entire group was modeling with clay. In subsequent conversations she expressed that she thought this type of sculptural modeling to be a truly artistic-therapeutic approach, giving the children a sense of deep calm and peace. She characterized it as an inner, active quietness. She considered the encounter between both whole hands and the material as an important factor in this process. She thought it essential to engage in such sculpting activities with children of this age, and felt that intense tactile experience guides the children towards their own sense of self, and through the healthy development of the tactile sense in childhood contributes decisively to a feeling of self worth in the human being. From her point of view sculptural modeling also enhances the stimulating and organizing effects of the will on the metabolic processes. In conclusion, she considers this method of sculptural modeling to be an important contribution to an accordant human and, therefore, healing education for the children.

VI

Excerpts by Rudolf Steiner Regarding Sculptural Modeling

with Notes by Hella Loewe

What follows are statements by Rudolf Steiner in regard to sculptural modeling, in conjunction with comments from the author. The quotations are organized, with one exception, in chronological order. They are offered in support of the pedagogical work outlined in this book and to place it appropriately in the overall context of Waldorf pedagogy. Abbreviated as these passages are, their full meaning can only come when read in the overall context of the respective lectures. In the lecture cycle *Art in the Light of Mystery Wisdom*, Steiner demonstrates in the area of pedagogy, the art of education, how terms of spiritual science can become alive in outer life. He sketches out the essential traits of a new pedagogy, which took living form nearly five years later with the founding of the first Waldorf school in Stuttgart.

"Now we turn the attention to the teacher. When we become teachers, our own next incarnation converses with the previous incarnation of our students. The teacher who has cultivated the right feeling says: 'Your best quality resides in you, it is what your mind can think, your soul can feel – it is this which is preparing itself in you in order to shape you for your next incarnation.' Only this attitude can work on the part of the child that is sculpting his form from time immemorial. The musical element in us is what enables us to educate.

"Take as a whole all that I have said in these lectures about the musical element and of how, in its most exalted form, it corresponds to what the human being meets with initiation. What we should educate in the child is the element of sculpture. That which we are supposed to impact is taking living form in the child. The musical element refers developmental, to things future, while the sculptural-architectural element refers to things past. The most wondrous sculptural, living work of art confronts us in the form of the child. We as educators are supposed to have a musical attunement, which can dwell in us as a mood of the future. Pedagogy will in future times be pervaded by the atmosphere of truth – when the world will gain insight as to how the musical attunement of the educator sets the pedagogical tone in conjunction with the sculptural [formative] embodiment of the student. It will then penetrate and the understanding will dawn that this is the true challenge of educational love, of pedagogic love. There is an educational force in this mood."[24]

On the founding of the first Waldorf school, Steiner held for the first faculty the lectures about the *Foundations of Human Experience* and *Practical Advice to Teachers* regarding the new art of education. An open conversational seminar and three comprehensive lectures about the curriculum followed. Between August 21 and September 6, 1919, the first teachers received this foundation for their work. We know these facts. But what is maybe not known to every teacher and to the readers is that, already on the first day of this introduction in the new pedagogy, Steiner emphatically pointed to the importance of cultivating the artistic element in the child. "The artistic element indeed does impact the will nature of the human being in a peculiar way. Through art we make contact with something intrinsically connected with the whole human being.

While the conventional approach [to teaching] only deals with man from a rational head-orientated standpoint, the methodological approach to our task will always involve targeting the whole being.[25] We not only want to avoid ever turning the capacity of will in the wrong direction because we use the wrong tools, but we want to strengthen and bring the willing faculty through artistic means to proper expression. This shall be brought about by offering right from the beginning lessons in painting, art and music. That is when we will notice that, particularly in the second seven-year period, the child is most receptive to authoritative instruction in things artistic, and that it is at that time we can be most effective in instructing them."[26]

So Steiner expected not only that the teachers would foster the artistic element in the child, but that the whole body of instruction should be drawn from the wellspring of art. "All methodical approaches must be dipped into the fountains of art."[27] This is a great challenge for the teacher!

The tasks still differ widely in content and yet are linked in regard to the goal. The teacher must train to become an artist. He is supposed to teach artistic things, art forms like sculptural modeling or drawing, and at the same time he is supposed to act as an artist of education by teaching in an artistic way such conventional subjects as writing and grammar.

Steiner returned to this theme of the artistic element two days later in his course on matters of method and didactics. Here he characterized two streams that impact the human being artistically: the sculptural-pictorial stream and the musical-poetic stream.[28] He said that these two diametrically contrasting energies could nevertheless well unite on a higher level. If we consider the entire body of Steiner's pedagogic lectures today, we can recognize how these two streams – the sculptural-pictorial and the musical-poetic elements – pervade Waldorf pedagogy like two life-giving arteries.

These statements made between August 1919 and August 1924 in regard to the sculptural-pictorial element in education, give us insight. His concept for the artistic instruction of first graders in the sculptural-pictorial area encompasses drawing (form drawing), watercolor painting, and sculptural modeling. These three elements form one balanced whole, harmonious triad. The artistic motif in form drawing is the line, straight or curved, one-dimensional, not representing anything in particular but allowing elementary forms to emerge on the plane, tracing a motion sequence. Color is the basis for working with watercolor paints. The artistic motif is the two-dimensional colored plane. In sculptural modeling, our artistic motif is three-dimensional – the planes with outward curvature (convex) or inward curves (concave) through which the spatial awareness of the children is exercised. Steiner emphasized in *Practical Advice to Teachers* that the goal is not to draw or model some *thing,*[29] not to imitate this or that, but to awaken in the child first an interest in pure, primal forms. "The similarity with the outer world must arise only as a secondary factor. It is the inextricable link with the form itself that has to live in the human being! We draw with the hand and we also model with the hand and yet both processes are entirely different. That can find a particularly clear expression when we bring children into the artistic realms. When we introduce children to the sculptural element, we have to take particular care to have them follow the modeled forms with their hands.

"While the child feels his or her own form-giving process by moving the hand and drawing something, we can also guide her in using the eyes to follow the forms with the will emanating through the eye. When we guide the child to trace the form of the body with her hollow hand, when we alert her to the way the eye follows the turns of a circle, for example, we do absolutely nothing that would hurt the innocence of the child. Rather, we fully rivet the interest of the entire human being."[30]

In a lecture four days later, Steiner emphasized the utmost importance of the first school lesson and gave a wonderful example of a conversation with children about the meaning of their school attendance. In the course of the dialogue, he also directed their awareness to the fact that they have hands, hands for working. Then he proceeded to let the children do something with their "skillful hands," first demonstrating it to them: "Now I do this. So take your hands and do the same." He drew a straight line. Steiner continued: "You can now let the children do the same, as slowly as possible, because it will proceed correctly. Indeed the proper assimilation of the lesson is of highest importance in this process. Later one can say to the child, 'Now I do this:' (Steiner drew a curved line.) 'Now you do that too, with your hand.' After that is done, you tell them, 'This is a straight line, and the other one is a curved line; so you just made with your hands a straight and a curved line.' The clumsy children receive help, but one should take care that each child does it right from the beginning with a certain perfection."[31] Even though this passage does not immediately refer to sculptural modeling, it gives us an important clue for the verbal and practical guidance of first grade children.

In his second *Lecture on Curriculum*, Steiner spoke about the curriculum for mathematics and geometry: "… and in the fourth grade drawing class we teach what a circle is, or an ellipse, and so forth. We teach this by starting with the drawing process. We further continue this process, definitively moving into sculptural modeling, by using plasticine – if we can get it. Otherwise we can use something else – and if it were street dirt – it doesn't matter! – in order to also develop the ability to see form and sense form, to make form sense emerge [from] form perception."[32] [This could also be translated: "to develop form-senses from form-perception."] And a little later he added: "Evoke the ability in the child to recognize the difference between a spherical and an ellipsoid curve. In short, awaken the form sense before the impulse to imitate goes into action! Do not let the child imitate anything before you have nurtured in him the inner sense for the form in its own dynamics, which can then later also be imitated. Follow the same principle, when you move to a more self-reliant treatment of drawing and painting and also to sculptural exercises."[33]

In the afternoon of the same day, in the third *Lecture on Curriculum*, Steiner added: "Sculptural modeling should begin *before* [emphasis by H.L.] the ninth year, first with spheres, then other forms, and so on. In modeling, too, one should work entirely out of the forms."[34] It is of far-reaching consequence that Steiner requires us to start with the sphere when modeling with the children. In the lecture titled "Architecture as a Synthesis of the

Arts," he expounds: "In the sphere form, the self – the 'I' – can be felt, if we proceed from the purely mathematical knowledge of form to sensing the form; then one will always experience the 'I,' the self, in the perfect circle. To feel the circle in a plane, the sphere in space, means to feel self, to feel the 'I.' You should clearly grasp that basically every really alive human being will feel the reference to a sense of being self-reliant, [even] when they see only a little bit of a spherical shape. The human being, if he feels like that, learns to live in forms. And it is so-to-say a characteristic of a vivid feeling faculty, if one can live in the forms."[35]

In May 1920 Steiner spoke in his lectures on *The Renewal of Education* about the importance of rhythm in children's education. Again the motif of the two polar streams within the artistic sphere is mentioned: "In the course of his life, the human being undergoes daily the change between sleeping and waking. We can gain some slight understanding of the creative living interplay between these two states when we point to two polarized forces which exert a great influence on the entire art of education and on the human life. These forces are polarized in drawing and in music, two contrasting elements that I have previously mentioned and that we want take a look at today from a special viewpoint. Let us look at the formative arts, among which I count painting, drawing and sculpting. Let us remember everything that was deemed necessary for the child in regard to the sculptural-pictorial arts right from the start of school. What does this formative art element show us? It shows us that the human being creates the form, which it finds in the outer world, from within his own nature. I have called attention to the fact that the goal is not to keep to an outer model, but that we have to find from within our own nature a feeling, a sense for form.

"But finally we have to become aware of how we create form in space in drawing, in painting and in that which is part of spatial form-giving. In all that, we are standing within an element that surrounds us in our waking state in the outer world. We draw lines, we paint colors, and we shape forms following examples. Lines appear to us, even though they do not appear as such in nature; but they take form for us through nature, just like colors and forms."[36]

In the second lecture of *Balance in Teaching*, Steiner characterized these forces which become operative in the body of the child starting with the seventh year. The following excerpt may serve as an inspiration to study it in its original context: "It is the change of teeth which is the physical expression of the battle between the two types of force, those forces which later emerge in the child as the powers of mind and intellect and those which have to find special expression in drawing, painting and writing. All the powers which shoot up here we use, when we develop writing abilities out of form drawing, because these forces actually want to transition into sculptural form-giving, into drawing, and so forth. These are the forces which find their end point in the changing of teeth. They previously formed the body of the child, the sculptural forces, and we make use of them later, after the change of teeth is over, in order to introduce the child to drawing, painting and so forth. These are mainly those forces which have been planted in the child by the spiritual world and in whose sphere the child's soul lived before conception. They act first as physical forces to develop the head center and then as soul-forces, starting with the seventh year. …That is the secret: These forces are connected to what we have already experienced between our death and our rebirth. That which we need in educational practice we can receive in awe, which can have a religious character, if we realize that the powers which you draw from the child around the seventh year, which you put to use in learning to draw or write, are ultimately sent by heaven. That means, the spiritual world sends down these forces, the child is the mediator, and the teacher actually works with the powers sent down from the spiritual world. This awe of the spiritual-divine is – when it streams down into the teaching process – indeed a miracle-generating force acting in the class. And when you have the feeling that you are connected to the forces that are taking form, drawing into manifestation – forces from the time before birth, from the spiritual world – when you have this feeling which generates a deep sense of reverence, then you will see that you can bring about more through the presence of that feeling than through all the intellectual scheming of what one should do.

"The teacher's feelings are the most important tools of education. And this reverence has a tremendously formative effect on the child."[37] After additional information about the effect of sculptural-architectural forces on one side and the speech-musical forces on the other side, Steiner continued: "If we become more reverent by fostering our connection and correspondence with the pre-natal powers, then we become more enthusiastic, enthusiastic for teaching based on the other forces of man which are growing more profound. A so-called Dionysian element radiates through the speech-music related lessons, while the sculpting, drawing and painting lessons receive a more Apollonian element. The lessons in the musical-speech sphere are taught through enthusiasm, the others we infuse with reverence.[38] Reverence and enthusiasm – these are the secret primordial forces, the two powers that can be considered necessary for spiritualizing the soul of the teacher."[39]

In the fourth lecture in *Balance in Teaching*, Steiner guides educators and teachers to understand the development of the human being, his entire soul organization based on the physical organization, arising from the peculiar characteristics and movements of the human form, guiding us to penetrate this mystery. "Coming to know children in this way can give us clues to strange things, if the teacher is a person who is inclined towards such a karmic understanding … and, oddly, it is true that if we meet the child like that, develop our love for the child, then we bring it into a state that allows us to understand it with ever greater love." Steiner then describes in this context, what it is that makes a person a sculptor, so we can understand that this not only applies to sculpting art, but as much to the art of education. "And one becomes a sculptor by learning to understand the organism and its forms, for example also in the form-giving arts. There is a totally different feeling at work when you as a sculptor form a human head than when you form the rest of the body. While shaping the head you all the time feel: the head affects you from within, you have to yield in forming the head; something pushes towards you from within. When you sculpt the rest of the body, you have the sense: you are pushing into the form, this part of the organism is yielding to you. There are two diametrically opposed feelings when shaping the head and when forming the rest of the

organism. This shows us how we need to learn the proper approach in all areas of work."[40]

In his so-called "Christmas Course" which he held for teachers in Dornach, Switzerland, Steiner first covered the basics of guiding the new first grade students towards painting with liquid colors; he then moved on to talk about modeling. He also mentioned modeling in connection with learning foreign languages. Again he pointed out how important it was that the children should be introduced to modeling at an early age, especially in the first phase of starting school. "And though it may be a hassle, one should really let the child form small objects … from materials you find somewhere. It is true that one should guard the children from soiling their hands and clothes; that is indeed a hassle. But what the children gain in that process is immensely more valuable than keeping the children from getting dirty. In short, especially during the early phases of schooling it is necessary to introduce the children to the artistic element. Everything that is to be expressed by the child must be brought towards the child in a manner suitable for the child. When we introduce the children to art in such ways, then the other subjects will proceed much easier. For example, they will have a much easier time learning languages if we acquaint them with art."[41]

In the lecture cycle "The Seasons as the Breath-Cycle of the Earth and the Four Great Festivals,"

Steiner tells us how the summer solstice festival, which became the St. John's Festival, and the winter solstice celebration, which became our Christmas, were observed in ancient times in connection with the ancient mystery teachings. "At the time of St. John's Festival everything was pervaded by the musical-poetic element, by the dance element [strictly rhythmically structured circle dances, accompanied by primitive instruments]. During the time of deepest winter, everything was being prepared for the human beings to realize they must become still, they must enter a more contemplative element… . Teaching proceeded in the winter months. And so the people were guided by the students of the mystery schools, starting at the time of our months of September and October, to engage in what we today would call guessing games, solving puzzles, also in throwing runes and interpreting the resulting forms. And they especially cultivated those forms of teaching which led to a certain primitive art of sculpting. When the harvest was over, and the limbs could rest, in them [the people] the need arose to do something; all limbs became desirous of kneading. A particular satisfaction was derived by everyone from sculptural forming. Just as an intense urge to dance, to open oneself to music, emerged around the time of the St. John's Festival, so around Christmastime, an intense urge sprang up to knead, to form something from all kind of pliable materials that were around – to form something, to also use all natural materials. In the time of deep winter, he [the human being] turned to the earthen element, and he tried out what kind of forms the earthen element could take on.

"From the sculpture, which he drew out from the natural dynamics of the earth, he arrived at the view that the earthen element virtually gives rise to the various animal shapes. At Christmastime the human being was able to understand animal forms. By working and exerting his limbs and by observing his natural surroundings, he noticed the form he had as a human being. But this happened only at Christmastime that the human came to know the earth, not at any other time. Around Christmastime the mystery teachers had the earth answer to the human questions by way of sculptural modeling, so that the people would slowly become interested in the human form, in the flowing together of all animal forms into the human form. Around Christmastime man came to know the Earth in its formative power, in its sculptural-pictorial power, and he learned to realize how at the time of St. John's, the time of high summer, the harmonies of the spheres resounded in his inner self through his dream awareness. And that is how the old mysteries expanded the human being at the special festive times of the year."[42] When we consider that the history of human development shows clear parallels to individual development, also of modern man, then we can conclude from the context of the passage just quoted that in the yearly cycle, the fall and winter seasons are most suited for teaching the children sculpting and modeling in clay.

A few weeks later, in May of 1923, Steiner spoke in Christiana (Oslo), Norway again about art and about the purpose anthroposophy intends to realize for art, artistic creativity and artistic perception. He talked about how life, how the living power of art, can be detached from the tools used by the various art disciplines. He spoke first about painting and the color experience, then proceeded to talk about sculptural-formative art. "In the dead medium of the picture, the Life Force appears to us in the plant through the color green. That is precisely what is so delightful, that life shows up in the dead picture. We only need to remember how the human form appears to us in the lifeless sculpture, and what makes it so attractive is that in the sculpture's dead image can appear like that which is alive; in dead, rigid forms life can be brought to expression. The same we observed with the color green."[43] He continued: "The poetic element wells up from fantasy. Fantasy usually just represents the unreal to people, that which one imagines, which is not there. But which force expresses itself in fact through fantasy? In order to understand the powers of fantasy, let us

regard the age of childhood. There is no fantasy yet in childhood. It at best knows dreams. The freely creative power does not yet dwell in the child. It does not live in the open. But fantasy is not something that suddenly emerges from nothingness. In fact, fantasy is hidden in the child even though it is not yet revealed, and the child is filled with fantasy. But how does fantasy work in the child? To him who can view the development with unencumbered spiritual eyes, it becomes apparent how in tender childhood the brain, as well as the rest of the organism, is still unformed in relation to the later body. On the inner plane, the child is the most incredible, eminent sculptor of his own organism. No sculptor is so wondrously able to create world forms from within the cosmos such as the child creates when he or she forms the brain and the rest of the organism in the time between birth and the change of teeth. The child is a wondrous sculptor, but it is the formative force, which works in the organs as an internal growth and form-giving energy."[44]

In August 1924 Steiner returned to these themes in a lecture in Torquay, England. He challenged the teachers to let the children engage in modeling and painting after the change of teeth because they have the urge to create form through sculpting and painting.

Speaking in Ilkley, England, in August 1923, about the founding and organization of the Waldorf school, Steiner remarked on the sculptural-pictorial element: "The focus on the sculptural-pictorial element is also apparent in the fact that we must develop writing from the drawing process. So, according to the principles of Waldorf education, we start already in earliest childhood with instructions in painting and drawing. Also the sculptural element is fostered wherever possible, however mostly starting at the age of nine or ten and in a primitive way. But if the child is also introduced to sculpting at the right age, we observe an enormously enlivening effect on the physical sense of vision, it ensouls the physical ability to see… . It is particularly valuable for this correct way of seeing to instruct the child as early as possible in sculptural activity, moving the visual impressions from the head region, from the eyes to the finger movements, into the hand movements."[45]

A little later in the same lecture, Steiner talked about the right way to gain insight and understanding for the world and how to learn to comprehend the various kingdoms of Nature: "If we want to comprehend the mineral kingdom, we can do so by contemplating cause and effect. That's how it can be understood on the physical plane. If we ascend to the plant kingdom, it becomes already impossible to understand everything through logic, mind and intellect. The form-giving element in the human being must become alive, concepts and ideas are transitioning into pictorial forms. And any form-giving skills we teach the child will enable her to comprehend the plant being by grasping its form. If we want to realize the nature of the animal kingdom, we can only approach this realization by predicating our terms of knowledge on our moral education… . And if we want to reach up into the human kingdom, we are in need of comprehensive artistic understanding."[46]

This remark shows us that the form-giving element should be practiced with the children as much as possible, because it is of profound importance for a living understanding, for a sensitive comprehension of the plant being and its organization. That seems to be the objective of Steiner's statements in this lecture with regard to sculptural modeling. It is somewhat puzzling that Steiner says that sculpting exercises should start only in the ninth or tenth year without giving a reason for this timeframe. This remark contradicts his statement in the *Third Curriculum Lecture* that "modeling exercises should start *before* the ninth year."[47] Perhaps the teaching experiences I have described here may help to resolve this contradiction.

All these statements explain *what* the children are supposed to learn and gain from sculptural modeling. There is only scanty reference to *how* the teacher should approach this task in the first grades methodologically and especially artistically. For example: "First spheres and then other forms… ." In the course discussions and in many pedagogical lectures after August 1919, Steiner gave numerous and differentiated methodological suggestions and practical examples for form drawing taken from teaching experience. In comparison, his references to sculptural methodology are scarce, and yet if we review the sum of all his statements we can recognize the sketch of an approach that we could take with the children. Steiner does guide the teacher on how to school herself in order to do justice to this artistic and educational task. In the last year of his pedagogical work, between April and August 1924, he quite obviously emphasized the importance of sculptural modeling: "When we immerse ourselves in sculptural modeling, then we know from within how to model a round form or a corner, how the inner forces create the shape that way. One cannot grasp the etheric body through what we generally consider to be natural laws. The etheric body is grasped with that which is given into our hand, into our spirit-permeated hand. Therefore, no teacher training should proceed without including artistic modeling and sculpting, which emerges from the inner world of the human being. When that element is missing, it has a much more unfavorable impact on education than if we do not know the capital of Romania … because that information we can look up in the encyclopedia … and there is no harm in looking that up. But there is no encyclopedia in the world in which we can learn that agility, that skillful knowing and knowing skill which we need to understand the etheric body, not proceeding according to natural law but pervading the human being through form-giving activity."[48]

A week later (April 13–17, 1924) in Bern, Switzerland, Steiner gave a pedagogical lecture course and again spoke at length about this subject: "One would have to really observe how the etheric body shows itself in the human being, for example. In order for a certain faculty to appear, we would need an entirely different type of college and university education, which should be mandatory both for educators in all fields as well as for medical professionals. This type of education would consist of learning first how to sculpturally model truly from within, from the wellspring of unfolding human nature. This would enable the students to create forms as an expression of their inner logic. You see, the form of a muscle or a bone is not knowable through an effort of will, an approach that prevails in today's anatomy and physiology. Forms are only grasped when we grip them through our form-giving faculties."[49] He then provided a detailed characterization of the etheric body in connection with the stellar influences in the cosmos and about the impact of cosmic forces on formation of the human muscular and bone systems. After that, he made statements directly addressed to sculptors and concluded: "We must be able to turn to the great cosmic sculptor, who creates form within the human being through spatial awareness. So that is what must be developed first: a feeling for space![50] If man only develops the physical senses, he does not develop this subtle spatial sensitivity. And a feeling for such tactile, explorative work with a soft, pliable material is the basis for understanding the etheric body. Similarly, the rational mind, being tied to the brain and to the sense organs, is the basis for understanding the physical body. We first have to create a methodology of knowledge; that means developing a sculptural awareness which is always somehow connected with inner form-giving activity. Otherwise the knowledge of the human being stops with the physical body, because the etheric body cannot be understood in concepts but only in images whose cosmic origin we only can comprehend through re-creating the form in some way."[51]

During the "Easter Course for Medical Students and Doctors" in Dornach, Steiner was asked a question about an approach to understanding the nature of the etheric element. In response, he suggested a modeling exercise to the participants. He talked about modeling the human form in five consecutive steps – starting from the sphere. He explained how convex protrusions are the result of the influx of cosmic forces, and that concave hollows, in contrast, are brought about by the densifying forces emanating from the center of the earth.[52]

Steiner talked to future teachers of the first English Waldorf school in Torquay, in what was to be the last pedagogical lecture series he was able to deliver. From his profound and comprehensive knowledge of man and with creative imagination, he resumed the subject of sculptural modeling: "Now we must realize that the autonomous activity of the human etheric body actually only starts with the change of teeth; we need to be clear about that. In the first seven years, all the etheric body's faculties for autonomous activity are fully engaged in shaping the second physical body. That means, the etheric body acts as a true inner artist within the child, a form-giver, a sculptor. This sculptural force applied by the etheric body to the physical body becomes autonomous in the seventh year of life with the first change of teeth; it emancipates itself, becomes free. After that, it can turn towards soul activity. That is why the child has the urge to create forms through modeling and painting. That is precisely what the etheric body did with the physical body in the first seven years: it sculpted and painted within. Now that it has no more work to do on the physical body, or just a little more, it can start to turn its activities outwards. You as a teacher may well know all the forms occurring in the human organism, and you also will know what forms the child likes to bring forth from within the sculpting materials, or what she likes to paint with colors. Based on this knowledge, you will also know how to give the child good instructions. Therefore it is definitively important that the teacher herself take up modeling in some form, because the current teacher training does not yet provide enough in this direction."[53]

Steiner then proceeded to give instructions for modeling organ shapes and suggested exploring anatomy through sculptural modeling in preparation for artistic work with the children. He pointed also to modeling in connection with human physiology in middle school, which has to be introduced by the teacher in a very special way. "If we just let the children engage in free form modeling, after having explained to them something about the human body, about a lung or any other organ, it is interesting to watch how they start, without conscious intent, to compose lung-shaped forms or something that resembles lungs. We can observe with interest how the child creates forms from within his own human beingness. This is why it is necessary that teachers really immerse themselves in this sculptural approach and look for ways to learn shaping the forms of the human organs in true correspondence to their purpose, using wax, plasticine, or anything else even if it is the 'mud from the side of the road,' as our children often do. Oh well, if we do not have any other materials, then mud is a very good medium."[54]

ENDNOTES

1. The original German word here is *plastizieren*, to plasticize; probably a word invented by Rudolf Steiner to describe sculptural modeling.

2. GA 294, p. 10, August 21, 1919 (Collected Works of Rudolf Steiner, vol. 294, p. 10).

3. GA 311, p. 96, August 18, 1924.

4. GA 295, p. 182, June 9, 1919.

5. See also Patzlaff, *Der Gefrorene Blick* [The Frozen View], 2001.

6. Patzlaff, p. 110.

7. GA 294, p. 19, August 21, 1919.

8. GA 286, p. 77, June 28, 1914.

9. Schuberth, 1985, p. 171.

10. GA 294, p. 19, August 21, 1919.

11. GA 295, p. 17, June 9, 1919.

12. GA 307, p. 176f., August 14, 1923.

13. GA 307, p. 180, August 14, 1923.

14. GA 303, p. 180ff., January 1, 1922.

15. GA 311, p. 98, August 18, 1924.

16. GA 294, p. 150f.

17. GA 295, p. 169, June 9, 1919.

18. GA 223, p. 67f., April 7, 1923.

19. Jünnemann, Weitmann, 1976, pp. 9 and 100.

20. GA 271, October 28, 1909.

21. Kranich, 2002.

22. Patzlaff, 2001, p. 110.

23. This is a verse that the teacher individually chooses for every single child when giving out the yearly reports for parents.

24. GA 275, p. 123f., January 2, 1915.

25. GA 294, p. 10f., August 21, 1919.

26. GA 294, p. 15, August 21, 1919.

27. GA 294, p. 11, August 21, 1919.

28. GA 294, p. 37, August 23, 1919.

29. Emphasis by H.L.

30. GA 294, p. 19, August 21, 1919.

31. GA 294, p. 56f., August 25, 1919.

32. GA 295, p. 169, September 6, 1919.

33. GA 295, p. 17, September 6, 1919.

34. GA 295, p. 182, September 6, 1919.

35. GA 286, p. 76, September 28, 1914.

36. GA 301, p. 171f., May 6, 1920.

37. GA 302a, p. 26ff., September 9, 1920.

38. GA 302a, p. 31, September 9, 1920.

39. GA 302a, p. 33, September 9, 1920.

40. GA 302a, p. 67f., September 22, 1920.

41. GA 303, p. 223f., January 3, 1922.

42. GA 223, p. 65ff., April 7, 1923.

43. GA 276, p. 132, May 20, 1923.

44. GA 276, p. 141f., May 20, 1923.

45. GA 307, p. 222, August 16, 1923.

46. GA 308, p. 53, April 4, 1924.

47. GA 307, p. 224, August 16, 1923.

48. GA 308, p. 53, April 10, 1924.

49. GA 309, p. 44, April 13–17, 1924.

50. GA 309, p. 46, April 15, 1924.

51. GA 309, p. 47, April 15, 1924.

52. Husemann, 1982, p. 32.

53. GA 311, p. 96f., August 18, 1924.

54. GA 311, p. 98, August 18, 1924.

BIBLIOGRAPHY

Husemann, Armin J. *Der musikalische Bau des Menschen, Entwurf einer plastisch-musikalischen Menschenkunde* (*The Harmony of the Human Body*), Stuttgart: 1982.

Jünnemann, Margrit and Fritz Weitmann. *Der Künstlerische Unterricht in der Waldorfschule – Malen und Zeichnen* (*Painting and Drawing in the Waldorf School*), Stuttgart: 1976.

Kranich, Ernst Michael. *Die Intelligenz der Hände – Hand-Arbeit und Gehirnentwicklung* (*The Intelligence of the Hands – Handwork and Brain Development*) in: *Erziehungskunst,* 66. Jg. Nr. 5, Stuttgart: 2002.

Patzlaff, Rainer. *Der gefrorene Blick* (*The Frozen View*), Stuttgart: 2001.

Schuberth, Ernst. *Geometrische und menschenkundliche Grundlagen für das Formenzeichnen* (*Geometrical and Anthropological Foundations for Form Drawing*) in *Formenzeichnen*, Stuttgart: 1985.

Steiner, Rudolf. *Architecture as a Synthesis of the Arts,* CW 286, New York: Anthroposophic Press, 1997.

_________. *Art as Seen in the Light of Mystery Wisdom,* GA 275, London: Steiner Press, 1984.

_________. *Balance in Teaching,* GA 302a, London: Steiner Press, 1972.

_________. *The Child's Changing Consciousness,* New York: Anthroposophic Press, 1996.

_________. *Discussions with Teachers,* GA 295, New York: Anthroposophic Press, 1999.

_________. *The Essentials of Education,* GA 308, London: Steiner Press, 1968.

_________. *The Foundations of Human Experience,* GA 293, New York: Anthroposophic Press, 2001.

_________. *How to Know Higher Worlds,* CW 10, New York: Anthroposophic Press, 2002.

_________. *Der Jahreskreislauf als Atmungsvorgang der Erde und die vier grossen Festeszeiten,* GA 223, Dornach: 1990.

_________. *The Kingdom of Childhood,* GA 311, New York: Anthroposophic Press, 1984.

_________. *Kunst und Kunsterkenntnis,* GA 271, Dornach: 1985.

_________. *Kunst im Lichte der Mysterienweisheit,* GA 275, Dornach: 1990.

________. *Das Künstlerische in seiner Weltmission,* GA 276, Dornach: 2002.

________. *A Modern Art of Education*, GA 307, London: Steiner Press, 1972.

________. *Practical Advice to Teachers*, GA 294, New York: Anthroposophic Press, 2002.

________. *The Renewal of Education*, GA 301, Forest Row, England: Steiner Schools Fellowship, 1981.

________. *The Roots of Education*, GA 309, London: Steiner Press, 1968.

________. *Soul Economy*, GA 303, New York: Anthroposophic Press, 1986.

Made in the USA
Middletown, DE
09 June 2020